Rome

Daniel Nolan

ten things to do

[1] Take a night tour of the Forum area to turn a great experience into a truly unforgettable one (*see p. 28*).

[2] Strain your neck looking up at Michelangelo's ceiling in the Sistine Chapel; the world's greatest artistic achievement (*see p. 131*).

[3] Wander into a church at random, and wonder at the fact that Rome has over four hundred of these places, and yes, they are all as beautiful as this.

[4] Visit the market in Campo dei Fiori to stock up on Italian herbs and spices that will miraculously transform you into a gastronomic genius on your return home (*see p. 115*).

[5] Chat with a friend on the Spanish Steps and soak in the view and the unique atmosphere of the Piazza di Spagna below (*see p. 76*).

[6] Drink an iced coffee on a sunny day outside the Pantheon, which with its vast dome has stood unchanged for 1,900 years (*see p. 104*).

[7] Picnic on the lawns of the Villa Borghese, between cultural trips to the park's magnificent museums (*see p. 80*).

[8] Enjoy a mouth-watering Italian ice cream while gazing at the Trevi Fountain, along with a thousand other of your fellow visitors to the Eternal City (*see p. 52*).

[9] Try something on in a couturier of your choice on Via Condotti: you will never wear a better-tailored garment, even if it finally stays in the shop (*see p. 92*).

[10] Fall in love...with the work of one of the three geniuses who helped to make Rome the beautiful city it is: Michelangelo (*see p. 150*), Bernini (*see p. 83*) and Caravaggio (*see p. 103*).

contents

About this guide

As you can see, we have divided Rome into five districts and the aim of this guide book is to enable you to have a great day out in any one of them. For each district first a short selection of the major **art** sights is given, then some other things to see **in the area**, followed by some ideas on the **eat** opportunities—from pizzas to fine Roman dining—rounded off with our shortlist of **shop** recommendations.

In the **practicalities** section that follows we set the scene with a brief introduction to the city of Rome, how to get around, its food and drink and where to stay. The **history** pages give an overview of the key events in this city's long and momentous life, while at the back of the book there is a **glossary** covering some of the art terms and key personalities referred to in this guide, as well as a comprehensive **index** to help you find what you are looking for.

There are excellent **maps** throughout, inside the front cover is a map of all Rome, clearly indicating where the detailed maps to each district are to be found at the beginning of their sections. The numbers (**1**) on the maps locate the cafés and restaurants described later in that section.

Enjoy Rome and do not hesitate to contact us with any views, recommendations or corrections: **www.blueguides.com**

practicalities

INTRODUCTION

Rome is a spectacular and fascinating city, and its ancient buildings, cobbled medieval streets and enchanting Renaissance domes provide a unique stage on which locals play out their daily dramas.

If this is your first time in Rome, you may be struck by how much you already know about the city founded by the twins Romulus and Remus, which would conquer the known western world and then fall into ruin, only to majestically rise again to become the important European capital it is today.

The millions who visit Rome each year are continuing a tradition which began over a millennium ago, when the Vatican established itself as the centre of the world's largest religious organisation, and amassed a collection of artistic masterpieces to match. Inspired by the ruins of the ancient Roman Empire that still occupy much of the city's centre, the architecture of Rome was enriched by the brilliance of Gian Lorenzo Bernini and Michelangelo, who always maintained that the ancient Pantheon was surely the work of angels.

Rome is also exceptional for the well-preserved state of its architecture, thanks to the city embracing the concept of conservation one century earlier than the rest of Europe, and becoming industrialised one century later: there aren't many places you can see archaeologists digging the ruins of an ancient site just metres away from the busy main road of a modern city.

It is not only the supremely rich ancient culture that makes the city so alluring, it is the streets to explore, the virtual impossibility of finding even an average coffee, a badly-tailored suit or a piazza without a gorgeous fountain: it is all of these things that make Rome so, well, Romantic.

PUBLIC TRANSPORT
Getting in from the airport
An express rail service connects Fiumicino airport with Termini railway station (*map p. 51, B8*) every 30mins from 6.30am–11.30pm (6am–11pm to the airport). A slower service leaves every 20mins (less often on Sun) between 6am and 11.20pm (5am–10.30pm to Fiumicino). At night, buses run from Terminal C to Tiburtina station (*see map on inside cover*) at 1.15, 2.15, 2.30 and 3.45.

From Ciampino airport, the Terravision coach service (www.terravision.it) departs from outside the arrivals hall every half hour (8.40am–12.20am) and takes 40mins. Buses from Termini to Ciampino leave from outside the Royal Santini Hotel (Via Marsala 22; *map p. 51, B8*) from 4.30am–7.30pm. Tickets can be bought (cash only) at the Royal Santini reception, Ciampino arrivals hall or online.

The metro and bus services 492 and 649 (or night bus 40N) go to the city centre from Tiburtina. Further rail information and bookings are available at www.trenitalia.it, or call 892 021 (199 166 177 from mobiles) between 7am and 9pm.

Getting around by bus and metro
Rome's transport system is operated by ATAC which has a journey planner at www.atac.roma.it. Metro, bus and tram tickets are available from ATAC machines, newsstands, tourist information centres and some bars.

Buses run from 5.30am–midnight, and bus stops have timetables posted with a list of lines and the stops on each line.

Rome's metro system only skirts the areas in this guide. Line A runs from 5.30am–9pm, after which it is replaced by a shuttle bus service until 11.30pm. Line B runs from 5.30am–11.30pm. Both services run an hour later on Sat night.

One of the advantages of Rome is that the major sights are easily accessible by foot if you have a comfortable pair of walking shoes. There are some pedestrianised areas and not too many hills which means that reliance on public transport is not essential.

ENTERTAINMENT
The daily newspaper *La Repubblica* has an English-language section every Thurs with information on the week's exhibitions, concerts and

guided tours. *Where* magazine is a monthly, English-language, free publication which is placed in many hotels around the city and has entertainment listings. For up-to-date online listings, click on the English section at www.romace.it. Also useful is www.inromenow. com.

SHOPS

Most shops are closed on Mon mornings. Supermarkets are a rare sight in central Rome, but there are some to be found. They are generally open 8–8 Mon–Sat, and for slightly shorter hours on Sun.

Spar, at Via Giustiniani 18b (*map p. 99, C5*), is close to the Pantheon and has a good deli counter. Despar, at Corso Vittorio Emanuele 42 (*map p. 98, C4*), has a good selection of cheeses, herbs, fresh bread, and fruit. The best supermarket in the Vatican area is Standa at Via Cola Di Rienzo 173, inside the COIN department store (*map p. 102, A4*).

Grocery stores are usually open 8.30–1 & 4–7.30 every day, except Thur afternoon and Sun.

FOOD & DRINK

'If ever a city articulated itself through its restaurants, it's Rome,' says the food writer Rowley Leigh. Rome's food is earthy, elemental, with simple flavours and, in some ways, surprisingly rustic for the cuisine of a sophisticated capital city.

During the Roman Empire decadent citizens indulged in lucullian banquets—named after the Roman citizen, Lucullus, who was famed for his elaborate feasts—gorging for days on such delicacies as larks' tongues. Today, it is offal—sweetbreads, oxtails and intestines—that make the most famous Roman dishes, such as *animelle d'agnello* (lamb sweetbreads) or *pajata in umido* (calf's intestines with milk stewed with tomatoes). Other idiosyncratic offerings are *spaghetti a cacio e pepe*, spaghetti prepared like a risotto with Rome's famous salty pecorino cheese, and a generous grinding of fresh pepper; *carciofi alla giudea*, 'Jewish artichokes' flattened and lightly fried, which highlight the influence of Jewish culture on Rome; or *puntarella*, the bitter chicory that is served with an anchovy, lemon juice and olive oil dressing.

However, Rome has never been able to feed itself. The need to provide its rowdy citizenry with subsidised grain dictated foreign policy

Abundant displays of food found in Rome

2,000 years ago resulting in Egypt, with the enormous, fertile Nile valley becoming a personal possession of the emperor. Likewise, wheat came from Sicily, Northern Africa provided supplies of olive oil, and Phoenician traders from what is now the Lebanon supplied vast quantities of saffron and pepper.

Today, too, the influence of ingredients and cooking from beyond Rome's immediate surrounding countryside is felt. There are the ubiquitous pizzas (originally from Naples), salamis and hams from the length and breadth of Italy, fresh pineapple grown in the south for dessert, while wines reflect the full range of the Italian wine renaissance over the last twenty years: powerful and expensive reds such as *Barolo* from Piedmont, full and fruity red wines from the prolific vineyards of Sicily and Puglia, and Frascati, the light white from pretty vineyards on Rome's southern fringes.

Recommended **restaurants** are given in each section of this book. Our favourite restaurants carry the Blue Guides Recommended sign: ■ (see www.blueguides.com for details). Categories are according to price per person for dinner, with wine:

€€€   €80
€€   €30–40
€   under €30

WHERE TO STAY

Rome has an excellent selection of accommodation ranging from exclusive hotels at exclusive addresses, to good value rooms in converted convents. It is possible to stay right in the heart of the city near the major sights, such as opposite the Pantheon or at the bottom of the Spanish Steps, or to find somewhere away from the crowds. A full listing of accommodation in all categories is available from Roma Turismo at 11 Via Parigi (*map p. 51, A6*) or on its website www.romaturismo.it.

In this section you will find only a selection of the accommodation available in Rome. Hotels that are particularly good (in terms of location, charm, value for money) carry the Blue Guides Recommended sign: ■ (see www.blueguides.com for details). The prices below are a guideline only for a double room in high season:

€€€	€300+
€€	€200–300
€	below €200

€€€ **Albergo del Senato.** *Piazza della Rotonda 73, T: 06 678 4343, www.albergodelsenato.it. 57 rooms. Map p. 99, C5.* The Pantheon is within metres of Albergo del Senato, with unsurpassed views of Piazza Navona from the bedroom windows. Its location in the centre of the city, and close to the major sights, makes it the perfect base, yet the hotel rooms themselves are surprisingly quiet. The pretty roof terrace overlooking the piazza is a relaxing spot to sit and enjoy the views, before or after dinner. A very popular hotel which is worth booking in advance.

€€€ **Hotel Forum.** ■ *Via Tor de' Conti 25–30, T: 06 679 2446, www.hotelforum.com. 78 rooms. Map p. 21, A1.* As its name suggests, this hotel is situated overlooking the ancient ruins of Rome's Forum. Converted from an 18th century Dominican monastery, the rooms are clean and bright, but it is the views over the Colosseum and Capitoline Hill which are worth the price, particularly from the roof garden restaurant.

€€€ **Hassler Hotel** and **Il Palazzetto.** *Piazza Trinità dei Monti 6, T: 06 699 340, www.hotelhasslerroma.com.*

Hassler 99 rooms; Palazzetto 4 rooms. Map p. 75, D2. In an unbeatable location at the top of the Spanish Steps, the Hassler is one of the most famous of Rome's luxury hotels. Roberto Wirth, the General Manager of the hotel, comes from a long-established hotel dynasty originating in Switzerland. This pedigree is apparent in all features of the hotel, from the panoramic restaurant to the tiny 15th-century palazzetto on the other side of Piazza Trinità dei Monti, which has been refurbished and is now home to the International Wine Academy of Rome, with tasting rooms, a wine salon, outdoor garden and the excellent Il Palazzetto Restaurant . The rooms, terraces and rooftop restaurant all have outstanding views over the Spanish Steps and the city.

€€€ Hotel d'Inghilterra. ◼ *Via Bocca di Leone 14, T: 06 699 811, www.hoteldinghilterra roma.it. 98 rooms. Map p. 50, A1.* A hotel with a star-studded past: Gregory Peck stayed here during the filming of Roman Holiday and declared it a favourite, as did Elizabeth

Courtyard dining at the Hassler Hotel

Taylor, Richard Burton and Ernest Hemingway. The hotel is discreet and secluded despite being in a prime position close to the Spanish Steps and the exclusive shopping streets of Via Condotti and Via Borgognona. The small English-style bar, frequented by locals as well as hotel guests, is renowned for its Martinis and Bloody Marys.

€€€ The Inn at the Spanish Steps. ■ *Via Condotti 85, T: 06 6992 5657, www.atspanish steps.com. 24 rooms. Map p. 50, A2.* A luxury guesthouse in

a chic location next to Caffè Greco and surrounded by the top fashion houses of Via Condotti. It is a well-loved hotel in the city centre with stylish rooms individually decorated by a local interior furnishings firm, Tenco (the best rooms face Via Condotti). It is the small details which characterise this hotel and make it so popular—the pots of colourful flowers on the sun terrace, the small gifts of champagne or perfume left in the room each afternoon, the snack buffet provided before evening

A room with a view: the penthouse suite at the Hotel d'Inghilterra

drinks, and the large jacuzzi baths. It is advisable to book well in advance.

€€€ Raphael. ◼ *Largo Febo 2 (Piazza Navona), T: 06 682831, www.raphaelhotel.com. 56 rooms. Map p. 99, B6.* Distinguished by its ivy-clad frontage, it is said that the Raphael is the most charming hotel in the city centre. An 18th-century palazzo with a 21st century interior; the sleek executive suites were designed by the renowned American architect, Richard Meier. The lobby and library are filled with art of all kinds, from pre-Columbian Mayan pottery to a display case of Picasso ceramics, while the multi-level roof terrace showcases the architecture of Rome—the dome of St Peter's is visible in the distance. Dinner, prepared by chef Jean François Daridon, on the terrace is a rare treat.

€€ Hotel Art. *Via Margutta 56, T: 06 328 711, www.hotel art.it. 46 rooms. Map p. 75, D2.* A modern, sleek alternative to the abundance of Renaissance palace conversions in Rome. Here, you enter the hotel through an ethereal tunnel which leads into a space-age reception area. Rooms are located on brightly coloured floors which make you feel you have been transported to a sci-fi film set rather than the centre of the Eternal City, while the bedrooms themselves are tastefully decorated in neutral shades. Formally a church, the hotel has incorporated some original features into its ultra-modern design, such as the frescoed vaulted ceilings in the Crystal Bar. The hotel occupies a wonderful location on Via Margutta, the artists' street (*see p. 94*), with Santa Maria del Popolo and the Spanish Steps very close by.

€€ Hotel Mediterraneo. *Via Cavour 15, T: 06 488 4051. www.romehotelmediterraneo.it. 267 rooms. Map p. 21, A3.* Built in the 1940s to a design by the prominent architect, Mario Loreti, this is a wonderful celebration of Art Deco architecture in the city. The interior design and furnishings reflect the original style with beautiful inlaid wood panelling depicting classical scenes, a grand marble staircase and intricate mosaics. The hotel is close to the Termini station, on the Esquiline Hill, from where there are beautiful views over the city, particularly from the penthouse suites on the tenth floor and the roof terrace restaurant.

€€ Portrait Suites. *Via Condotti 63, T: 06 693 80742, www.rome-suites-portrait.com. 14 suites. Map p. 50, A2.* A luxurious B&B-cum-museum-gallery, the recently opened Portrait Suites is part of the Ferragamo fashion empire. On the main shopping street in Rome, at the bottom of the Spanish Steps, the suites are set above the Salvatore Ferragamo Men's Store and in keeping with the upmarket fashion brand, the furnishings are stylish and modern, with luxurious sofas on the roof terrace, and 14 individually designed suites. The communal areas are elegantly filled with photographs and memorabilia of Salvatore's illustrious career in which he clothed, among others, Elizabeth Taylor and Audrey Hepburn.

€ Hotel Bramante. ◼ *Vicolo delle Palline 24, T: 06 688 06426, www.hotelbramante.com. 16 rooms. Map p. 120, B3.* A friendly, family-run hotel in a quiet lane just off the Borgo Pio, a bustling stretch of restaurants, shops and hotels close to St Peter's. Housed in a 15th century building, where the architect Domenico Fontana used to live, the Mariani family have carefully converted the space into an intimate and beautifully decorated hotel. Many of the rooms have beamed ceilings and pale stone floors. Particularly good breakfast.

€ Il Covo. ◼ *Via del Boschetto 91, T: 06 481 5871, www.vogliadiroma.it. 15 rooms. Map p. 21, A2.* Il Covo bed and breakfast is located in the newly chic Monti district between Termini station and the Colosseum with some great shopping and eating opportunities (*see p. 46*). The rooms, which are not extravagant but are clean and furnished in a typically Roman style, each with a private bathroom and fridge, are located in different apartment buildings close to each other. Breakfast is served in the Bottega del Caffè in the pretty Piazza Madonna dei Monti. The accommodation is extremely good value for money given its location.

€ Hotel Gregoriana. ◼ *Via Gregoriana 18, T: 06 679 4269, www.hotelgregoriana.it. 19 rooms. Map p. 50, A3.* Originally a convent, the Hotel Gregoriana has been converted into an exceptionally neat hotel with just 19 single and double rooms. The owner, Aldo, has meticulously refurbished the rooms in an Art Deco style with beautiful inlaid furniture and marble bathrooms. The rooms are not large but all are spotlessly clean and light with large windows onto the quiet street outside. There is no restaurant; breakfast is served in your room.

The staff are particularly friendly and Aldo is an excellent source of local information. The location is fabulous: at the top of the Spanish Steps but tucked down a side street away from the evening crowds.

Hostels, apartments & convents

A number of convents offer well-located, well-priced accommodation and not just for nuns: they do accommodate women alone or in groups: the website of the American Catholic Church in Rome has a list (www.santasusanna.org/comingToRome/convents.html). Alternatively, there is www.hospites.it, an Italian website for religious houses across the country, partially in English but harder to navigate. If you are considering a stay in a convent, you need to be aware of each establishment's curfew to avoid being locked out for the night. The Suore di Santa Elisabetta convent in Via dell'Olmata just off Piazza Santa Maria Maggiore (*map p. 51, D6*) offers double rooms with bath and breakfast, Tel: 06 488 4066.

Hotel Campo de' Fiori has 15 apartments, all with one bedroom, living room and kitchen, accommodating up to four people with sofa bed and/or rollaway. Breakfast is included. Tel: 06 688 06865, www.campodefiori.com. Also www.apartmentsapart.com, with a dozen or so apartments in the centre of Rome. Hostels Alessandro has been operating in Rome for over ten years, and has three properties, all close to the Termini Station: the Alessandro Palace Hostel, the Alessandro Downtown and Alessandro Legends. All have a selection of double, triple, quad and dorms with up to ten beds, segregated for male and female travellers. The rates include breakfast, linen, free maps. Tel: 06 446 1958, www.hostelsalessandro.com

history

Roman Kingdom and Republic

1000-800 BC Rome probably inhabited by a Bronze-age civilisation

753 BC Romulus founds Rome, according to legend

753–509 BC Era of the Seven Kings of Rome, rulers drawn from Sabine, Latin and Etruscan stock

509 BC The Etruscan Tarquinius Superbus, last king of Rome, is run out of the city and the Republic is established

396 BC Rome consolidates its territory and wins battle against Etruscan city of Veii

246–146 BC Punic Wars fought by Rome against the Carthaginian general Hannibal. Rome gains control of Sicily, parts of Spain and north Africa

44 BC Julius Caesar murdered on the Ides of March and cremated in the Forum (*see p. 32*)

31 BC Octavian (later Augustus), Caesar's adopted son, ends the struggle for power when he triumphs over the forces of Mark Antony and Cleopatra

Roman Empire

27 BC–AD 14 Octavian (now known as Augustus, 'the revered one') establishes the Roman Empire, with himself as emperor, and brings peace to an unsettled realm

64 Great Fire of Rome under Nero

65 St Peter martyred under Nero, and buried on the site of the present St Peter's Basilica

68–117 Flavian dynasty (Vespasian, Titus, Domitian, Nerva and Trajan). Colosseum built

96–180 Era of the 'Five Good Emperors': Nerva, Trajan, Hadrian, Antoninus Pius and Marcus Aurelius maintain the Pax Romana (era of peace) that began under Augustus

125 Pantheon constructed by Hadrian as a temple to all the gods, later to become the first Roman temple to be Christianised, in 609 (see p. 104)

3rd century Crisis of the Roman Empire as marauding barbarian hordes stalk its frontiers. The Aurelian walls are built to protect Rome

312 Constantine defeats the rival emperor Maxentius at the Milvian Bridge on Rome's northern outskirts. Before the battle he had a vision of a heavenly Cross; after his victory he converts to Christianity, starts to build Christian basilicas in Rome, and makes Byzantium the new capital of the Empire

395 The vast Empire splits into two halves, the Western and the Eastern Empires

410 Rome sacked by the Goths under Alaric

476 The last Emperor of the West, Romulus Augustulus, abdicates and Rome is taken over by the Goths; its population falls

Medieval Rome

800 Charlemagne, King of the Franks, is crowned Holy Roman Emperor giving him, along with the pope, supreme rule over the Empire

846 St Peter's sacked by the Saracens

1300 Pope Boniface VIII proclaims first Holy Year

1309 Pope moves to Avignon under pressure from the French king. As the Catholic church splits, the competing line of papal pretenders in Rome are known as 'antipopes'

1374 Cola di Rienzo attempts a popular revolt, with the aim of reviving the ancient Republic, but loses support and is later killed

1377 The official pope and the Holy See return to Rome

The Renaissance and Baroque

1503–13 Julius II founds the Swiss Guard, and commissions Michelangelo to paint the Sistine Chapel ceiling (*see p. 131*)

1555 Creation of the Ghetto

1600 Giordano Bruno burned for heresy at the Campo dei Fiori

1626 New St Peter's Basilica consecrated

1655–67 The reign of Alexander VII sees the completion of St Peter's by his chief architect Gian Lorenzo Bernini (*see p. 83*)

1732 The commission for the Trevi Fountain is given to the little-known architect Niccolò Salvi, the construction of which was completed thirty years later

Modern Rome

1797 Napoleon Bonaparte leads the French armies into Rome

1808–14 France formally occupies Rome

1849 Republic of Italy established by Mazzini and Garibaldi in Rome, only for French troops to regain control of the city later that same year

1864 Italian troops secure Rome after the French troops leave to fight the Franco-Prussian war

1871 Rome is proclaimed capital of the new Kingdom of Italy. Pope Pius IX no longer wields temporal power and is confined to the Vatican

1922 Mussolini marches on Rome and seizes power

1929 Mussolini signs the Lateran Pact with Pope Pius XI, in which Italy recognises independent papal sovereignty over the Vatican City, and the Papacy in turn acknowledges the state of Italy, with Rome as its capital

1960 Rome hosts the XVII Olympic Games

1960 Federico Fellini directs *La Dolce Vita* in which Anita Ekberg famously wades in the Trevi Fountain (*see p. 52*)

1993–2001 Tenure of Rome's first directly-elected mayor Francesco Rutelli

THE FORUM

introduction

The Roman Forum, an extraordinary archaeological site at the heart of a modern metropolis, contains remains of the monuments and administrative buildings of an empire that stretched from Spain to Asia Minor. It is overlooked by the Palatine Hill, a former residential district for Roman patricians, and the Capitoline Hill, the site of Rome's most important temple to the king of all the gods, Jupiter, and now host to three magnificent treasure troves of art: Palazzo dei Conservatori, Pinacoteca Capitolina and Palazzo Nuovo, which share a square designed by Michelangelo.

The immense Colosseum, perhaps the greatest symbol of Rome, and the Arch of Constantine nearby, reflect the glory of the Imperial era, while Emperor Nero's palace, the Domus Aurea, displays its excesses.

Michelangelo's awe-inspiring sculpture of Moses is in the church of San Pietro in Vincoli. Other churches featured here are San Clemente, where visitors can descend from the upper church into an excavated 2nd-century temple; the one-time Papal seat of St John Lateran, still the mother church of the Catholic faith, and Santi Cosma e Damiano, which overlooks the Roman Forum and has mosaics from the early 6th century.

Trajan's Column, the Imperial Fora and the monument to King Vittorio Emanuele II–Rome's greatest architectural folly–are also included.

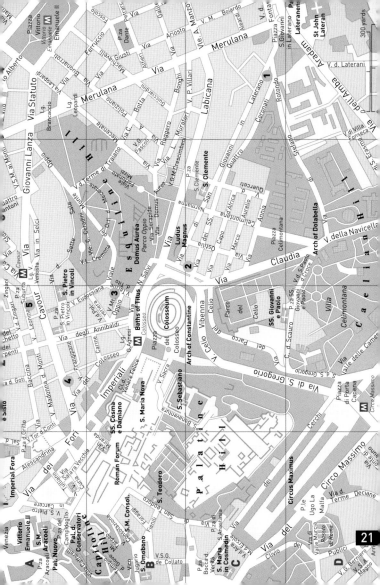

CAPITOLINE HILL

The Capitoline Hill (*map p. 21, B1*) is the ancient centre of Rome and because of that the most logical place to begin a trip around the city. Romulus, the city's founder, built his first fortress here in 753 BC. No trace of that remains. The main piazza you see today was laid out in 1538 by Michelangelo, who devised the oval star-design pavement and the elegant base of the bronze statue of the emperor Marcus Aurelius (*see p. 25*), although he disagreed with its final positioning. Since its restoration, the real statue has been situated inside Palazzo dei Conservatori in a purpose-built, glass-walled room , and was replaced here by a copy in 1997. The palace's Roman sculptures actually form the oldest public art collection in the world, founded by Pope Sixtus IV (the same pope who built the Sistine Chapel) in 1471. The museums contain numerous masterpieces and are an excellent introduction to Classical sculpture. The tranquil rooms have a unique atmosphere, especially in the evening, when they are lit by chandeliers.

Palazzo dei Conservatori

Open: 9–8, closed Mon **Charges:** Entry fee **Entrance:** Ticket office to the right of statue, entrance next door **Tel:** 06 3996 7800 **Map:** p. 21, A1
Highlights: Statue of Constantine the Great; She-wolf of Rome; Equestrian statue of Marcus Aurelius; *Gipsy Fortune-teller* and *St John the Baptist* by Caravaggio

This beautifully proportioned building by Michelangelo has a very unusual design, in which architraves (horizontal stone beams) replace the more usual arches to form an open gallery. In the courtyard are fragments of a colossal seated **statue of Constantine the Great**—who was proclaimed *augustus* by his troops in modern-day York, England, in 306, and ruled until 337—which was originally located at the Basilica of Maxentius in the Roman Forum. This is the definitive portrait of the emperor, with hooded eyes and curved nose. The head, hands and feet survive because they are of stone; the rest of the body would have been wooden.

The sculpture collection

In the ancient heart of the building, the Sala degli Orazi e Curiazi, two statues face each other: one in marble depicting Urban VIII, begun by Bernini, and another of Urban's successor Innocent X, made in bronze about ten years later by Bernini's rival Alessandro Algardi. The frescoed walls depict scenes from the history of Rome's origins. The Treaty of Rome founding the EEC was ratified in this room in 1957, and the EU constitution was signed here in 2004.

One of the most famous pieces in the collection is the **She-wolf of Rome**, an Etruscan bronze of the late 6th or early 5th century BC. This ancient piece carries a huge emotional weight, and her jutting ribs reflect the city's difficult and brutal birth. The She-wolf is mentioned in the writings of Pliny and Cicero, from the days when it stood on the

The Etruscan She-wolf of Rome with the infant twins, Romulus and Remus

Capitoline Hill, and has been displayed here since the 16th century. The wolf has been the symbol of the city from its earliest days: according to legend she found the abandoned baby twins Romulus and Remus and brought them up. Romulus later killed Remus and became the first king of Rome. The figures of the twins on the statue were added c. 1509. Another much-reproduced work (in the preceding room) is the *Spinario* (1st century BC), a sculpture of a boy removing a thorn from his foot. The work was once thought to depict Marcius, a Roman messenger, who carries on with his labour in spite of the pain. It was extremely influential and frequently imitated during the Renaissance.

In Room 5 is a bronze bust of Michelangelo, the definitive portrait of the artist by his close friend Daniele da Volterra. It was made from his death mask and clearly shows his broken nose, which he got in a fist fight during his youth from an envious fellow artist. In the next room is a marble head of Medusa by Bernini. The stairs to the left after Room 7 lead up to a café with a truly exceptional view over the city which is well worth the three-minute detour.

Room 10 has a well-preserved, exquisitely realised half-length portrait of the Emperor Commodus. An unpopular and conceited ruler, he is shown as he liked to be portrayed, in the guise of Hercules. The room connects to a glass-walled covered courtyard built to house the bronze **equestrian statue of Marcus Aurelius** (*see box opposite*).

The paintings

The Pinacoteca Capitolina gallery was established in 1749 and is significant for the 16th–18th-century Italian and foreign works which it houses. There are three paintings by Guido Reni, a High Baroque artist who was in great demand during his lifetime, and held to be the greatest of the era's painters until he fell from fashion at the end of the 19th century. His *St Sebastian* was called 'the most beautiful of all paintings' by the writer and wit Oscar Wilde. Reni focuses on the spiritual aspect of the saint's martyrdom and the delicate work has come to be considered something of a gay icon. The *Gipsy Fortune-teller* in Room 7 is an early Caravaggio genre painting (c. 1598). Here, the viewer can really get up close to the work, and marvel at the mastery of light. The foppish boy fails to notice that the woman is removing his ring, and the unwieldiness of the boy's sword adds to his appearance of naivety.

The statue of Marcus Aurelius

This Roman bronze masterpiece is thought to date from the latter
part of the philosopher-emperor's reign (AD 161–80). Few surviving Roman statues demonstrate the propaganda power of the
ruler as acutely as this one; it portrays him without weapons, as a
bringer of peace. In late antiquity the statue was wrongly thought
to portray the Christian emperor Constantine the Great. Because
of its value as a symbol of the new, triumphant religion, it was
preserved intact, and is the only Roman bronze of its era to have
escaped the ignominious fate of being melted down to make
coins or new statues. Many famous works, originally in bronze,
were copied in marble by later artists: marble cannot support its
own weight as well as bronze: figures leaning against tree stumps
or other supports are a tell-tale sign that the work is a marble
copy of an original in bronze. Few bronzes survive, which is what
makes this statue of the emperor so rare.

Caravaggio's other masterpiece here is an iconographically innovative painting of **St John the Baptist**, from 1602. The nude youth with the ram and the grapes is not obviously identifiable as the man who heralded the coming of the Messiah and ate locusts in the desert. In fact John the Baptist was traditionally depicted with a lamb, but for Caravaggio, who subverts the image here, he is often portrayed as a raw youth lost in the wilderness: perhaps the untamed artist identified with the saint. The gorgeous rendering of cloth, flesh and plants captures nature in full bloom, while the engaging yet ironic look of the subject adds to its allure.

Palazzo Nuovo

Open: 9–8, closed Mon **Charges:** Entry fee **Tel:** 06 3996 7800
Map: p. 21, A1
Highlights: *Capitoline Venus* statue; *Dying Gaul* statue

Designed by Michelangelo to match Palazzo dei Conservatori opposite, Palazzo Nuovo was built in 1644–55. It contains a superb collection of ancient Roman sculpture begun by the wealthy pope Clement XII, who also commissioned the Trevi Fountain.

Tucked away in the Gabinetto della Venere at the end of the gallery is the celebrated **Capitoline Venus**, which was found on Viminal Hill to the north of the Forum in the 17th century, and purchased by Pope Benedict XIV in 1752. Of marble from the Greek island of Paros in the Aegean Sea, it is thought to be derived from the Aphrodite made by Praxiteles for a temple on Cnidos in Asia Minor (modern-day Turkey), and is one of the most famous Greek statues. Praxiteles' model is thought to have been a courtesan named Phryne, who grew so wealthy thanks to her extraordinary beauty that she offered to rebuild the walls of Thebes as long as the words 'destroyed by Alexander, restored by Phryne the courtesan' were inscribed upon them. The goddess of love is taken by surprise before taking the ritual bath to restore her virginity, and shyly attempts to cover her nudity.

In the Sala Imperatori (Room 4), to the right of the entrance to

Room 5, is a magnificent collection of portrait busts, including one of Caesar Augustus, with his wife Livia alongside. Displayed on a pedestal is Marcus Aurelius as a handsome teenager, long before he became emperor; the bust on the top shelf opposite shows him at least 30 years later, by which time he had been worn down by the cares of state. It is interesting to note that of all the Imperial figures, only Marcus Aurelius—here on the upper shelf to the left of the entrance—is ever depicted exhibiting inner turmoil. On the lower shelf on the far right wall of Sala dei Filosofi is the mathematician Pythagoras.

In Sala del Gladiatore is the **Dying Gaul**, an exquisite work of a moustachioed Celtic warrior, naked except for a torque around his neck. It is a Roman marble copy of a bronze Greek original now lost. The original Greek statue was commissioned to commemorate a victory in Asia Minor in 239 BC over the invading Gauls, who frequently fought in a state of undress. The doomed warrior battles against his fate with great pathos, thus reflecting the might of the Romans who defeated him.

Santa Maria in Aracoeli

Open: 9–12.30 & 2.30–5.30 **Charges:** Free entry **Map:** p. 21, A1
Highlight: Cosmatesque floor

This tranquil 12th-century church, behind Palazzo Nuovo on the highest point of Capitoline Hill, was founded before the 8th century. It features a lovely **Cosmatesque floor** (*see box overleaf*), and in the nave are 22 ancient Roman columns of various different marbles, which were taken from pagan buildings. Facing the high altar are two beautiful marble pulpits decorated by the Cosmati family (c. 1200). Another Cosmatesque work is the handsome tomb of Cardinal Matteo di Acquasparta, which incorporates a fresco by Pietro Cavallini. The last chapel on the right is also by Pietro Cavallini and has a *Madonna and Child with two Saints* and *Christ between two Angels* from the late 13th and early 14th centuries, very rare examples from that predominantly lost era of Roman art.

a/s/e Rome

The 'Cosmatesque'

This attractive and innovative style of exquisite geometrically patterned cladding for walls, floors and other surfaces using fragments of discarded ancient Roman marble was developed in the 12th and 13th centuries. It was introduced to Rome through Laurentius of Anagni, who had learned under Greek masters, but soon broke with Byzantine tradition to create a vibrant and highly original style. It became known as the Cosmatesque, after its greatest practitioners, the Cosmati family. Over four generations seven members of the family produced it. Their work is principally found in Rome (for example in the cloister of St John Lateran; *see p. 43*), but became fashionable all over Europe: there are two Cosmatesque pavements in Westminster Abbey. The term now refers to work of this style by any of the anonymous craftsmen who practised the technique.

The Roman Forum

Open: 8.30–dusk **Charges:** Free entry **Tel:** 06 399 6700 **Map:** p. 21, B1–B2. *The Forum is sometimes floodlit on summer nights, and tours are available: for information call the number above.*
Highlights: Arch of Septimius Severus; Curia Julia (Senate house); Basilica of Maxentius

In the days of the Roman Republic (509–27 BC) the Roman Forum was an open area with shops and a scattering of temples, but from the 2nd century BC it became home to the grandiose public buildings and law courts of an Imperial capital. It remained the living, beating heart of the Empire for over half a millennium, during which time it was often embellished and added to. Today, the remaining ruins surround and tower over the seemingly endless trail of visitors to this site. Highlights are given below, and marked on the plan on pp. 30–31.

The three surviving columns of the Temple of Castor and Pollux

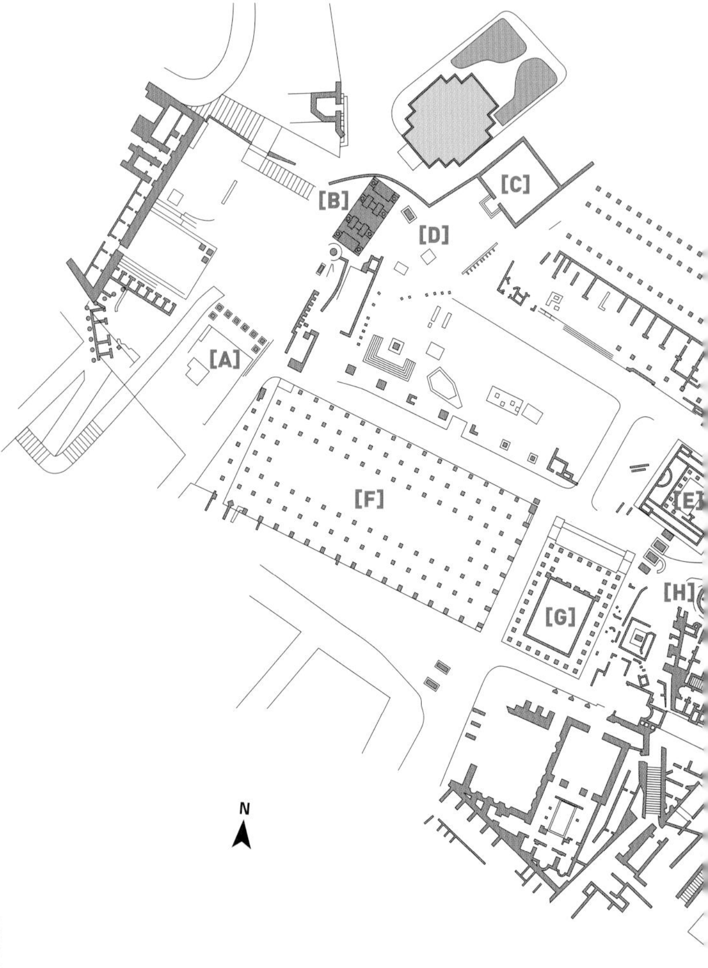
[A]
[B]
[C]
[D]
[E]
[F]
[G]
[H]
N

The Roman Forum

[A] Temple of Saturn
[B] Arch of Septimius Severus
[C] Curia Julia
[D] Lapis Niger
[E] Temple of Julius Caesar
[F] Basilica Julia
[G] Temple of Castor and Pollux

[H] Temple of Vesta
[I] Temple of Antoninus and Faustina
[J] Temple of Romulus
[K] Basilica of Maxentius
[L] Arch of Titus

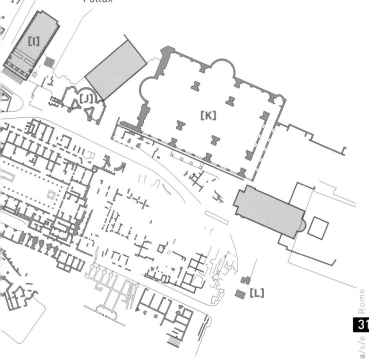

[A] Temple of Saturn: Six 11m columns in grey granite, and two in red, survive from the Temple of Saturn. The 'Saturnalia' was the most important day of festivities in the Roman year, when temporary freedom was given to slaves and gifts were exchanged. In later centuries this winter festival became associated with Christmas and New Year's Day. The temple was rebuilt in 42 BC, and the columns we see today survive from this time.

[B] Arch of Septimius Severus: This triple triumphal arch (AD 203) was erected to celebrate the emperor's victory over the Parthians (present day Iranians). Four large carved reliefs show scenes from the battles. Carved winged personifications of Victory flank the central arch. Around the base of the columns are carvings of Roman soldiers (with sandals and curly hair) leading Parthian captives (typically bearded and with caps on their heads; *see illustration on p. 19*).

[C] Curia Julia: this is the site of what is probably Roman official-dom's oldest meeting place, dating from the 7th century BC. The present building dates from the time of Domitian (AD 51–96) and was restored by Diocletian (c. 245–c. 312). The side walls with niches were partly faced with marble, and the floors remain richly decorated. The headless statue of Hadrian or Trajan exhibited here, dating from the 1st or 2nd century AD, was found in recent excavations behind the building. The Curia's original doors were replaced in the 17th century and now serve as the main doors at St John Lateran (*see p. 43*).

[D] Lapis Niger: protected by upright marble slabs and a modern iron fence this was a black marble pavement, laid to indicate a sacred spot, and is the site of some of the oldest relics of the Forum. To the left as you exit the Curia, are the remains of the paving stones of Argiletum, the busy street that led north to the Subura district, a rough part of town, described by Juvenal as home to 'the thousand dangers of a savage city'.

[E] Temple of Julius Caesar: On the right, along the Forum are the remains of the Temple of Julius Caesar, today just a curved wall protected by a roof. However, this is where Caesar's body was brought after his assassination on the Ides of March in 44 BC, and it was probably here that his body was cremated and his will read out by Mark Antony. The paved road in front of the temple is the oldest street in Rome: the Sacra Via. It runs the length of the Forum and was the road along which the victorious Triumph processions (*see box on p. 36*) marched on their way to the Temple of Jupiter on the Capitoline Hill.

[F] The **Basilica Julia** was begun by Julius Caesar in 54 BC. A circle and some letters etched into the stone on the marble steps mark where Roman citizens once

gambled and played games here.

[G] Temple of Castor and Pollux: Three tall columns are all that survive of this temple, built in 484 BC in honour of the twin sons of Jupiter. Romans of the equestrian class regarded them as their patrons and staged a parade in front of the temple on 15th July every year. The building was also used by money-changers, according to the Roman statesman and orator Cicero.

[H] Temple of Vesta: These reconstructed remains were once

Ancient evidence of game playing at the Forum

a circular temple where the Vestals tended the sacred fire and the goddess Vesta protected it (*see box below*). Behind this, to the southeast, was the House of the Vestals or *Atrium Vestae*, a three-storey, 50-room palace built around an elegant elongated atrium or court. Inside are remains of the statues of Rome's priestesses, dating from 3rd century AD.

[I] Temple of Antoninus and Faustina: This is one of the Forum's best-preserved temples.

It was a famous temple of Imperial Rome–which the Senate dedicated to the memory of Empress Faustina after her death in AD 141, and later to her husband Antoninus as well. It is thought to have been the site of St Lawrence's death sentence (he was sentenced to be roasted alive) in the 9th century. The temple had been converted into a church by the 12th century, and was given its Baroque façade in 1602.

The Vestal Virgins

Six Vestals were chosen by the king, and later by the emperor, to keep alight the fire symbolising Rome's perpetuity–its extinction would mean the fall of the state. Girls of great beauty between six and ten years of age were eligible if they had two living parents. After her election, a Vestal lived in the House of the Vestals for 30 years: for a decade learning her duties, for ten years carrying them out and for a further ten instructing novices. Due to the importance given to their task, they enjoyed many privileges, including the freedom to vote and to own property, and were held in such high regard that they could give evidence without first taking an oath. Wills–including the emperor's–and treaties were entrusted to them. During her 30-year tenure, the Vestal was bound by a vow of chastity; afterwards she was free to return to the world and to marry if she so desired. However, if a Vestal Virgin broke her vow of chastity, she was buried alive in Campus Sceleratus, the present Piazza Indipendenza (*map p. 51, A8–B8*), and her lover was whipped to death in the Forum. Over eleven centuries, at least 22 Vestals were accused of breaking their vow.

[J] Temple of Romulus: the so-called Temple of Romulus is a 4th-century building, and the best-preserved pagan building in Rome after the Pantheon. Extraordinarily, it still has its original ancient Roman bronze doors. A recent theory holds that it may actually have been a temple to Jupiter, or the city prefect's audience hall. It was converted into the church of Santi Cosma e Damiano (entrance from the other side; *see p. 42*) in the 6th century, the temple serving as a vestibule. The interior can be seen from the church.

[K] Basilica of Maxentius: At 100m long, 65m wide, and with vaults of 39m this gargantuan basilica was once the Forum's largest building. Its construction was started by Maxentius in 308, and completed in 325 by Constantine, the victor at the Battle of the Milvian Bridge (*see p. 17*). Its mammoth proportions reflect the growing insecurity of an increasingly divided Empire desperately trying to project an image of invincibility with ever-more vainglorious buildings. In the 4th century a basilica was actually a court, council chamber and meeting hall. The building originally housed the Emperor Constantine statue now in the courtyard of Palazzo dei Conservatori (*see p.22*). Michelangelo studied the basilica closely when designing the dome of St Peter's.

[L] Arch of Titus: At the high point of the Sacra Via is the imposing Arch of Titus, erected in honour of the victories of Vespasian and Titus that led to the sack of Jerusalem in AD 70. The perfectly-proportioned single archway has been a huge influence on triumphal arches across the world since the 16th century. The two reliefs show the goddess Roma with Titus, the winged figure of Victory, and a triumphal procession bringing war treasures from Jerusalem, including the altar of Solomon's Temple and the seven-branched golden candlestick (Menorah), the symbol of Judaism. The view of the Forum from underneath the arch is extraordinary, and perhaps the best place to imagine the ancient site in all its Imperial glory.

Triumphs

The Triumph ritual originated with the Etruscans before being adopted by the Roman Republic as a way of allowing generals to celebrate victory without being given any lasting political power. Once a major battle had been won the victor gathered his troops, captives and spoils outside the walls of Rome. Dressed as the god Jupiter, he then led the procession into the city through the southern gate in the walls and would enter the Forum and move along Sacra Via and up to the Temple of Jupiter on Capitoline Hill to place a laurel wreath and offer sacrifice to the gods. After his Triumph a general was supposed to retire from active political life, but towards the end of the Republican era, men such as Pompey the Great and Julius Caesar were bending these rules and a triumph became a stepping stone to more enduring power. So many generals applied for triumphs that it was later stipulated that 5,000 enemy soldiers had to have been killed in a victory which had effectively brought about the end of a war.

The Colosseum

Open: 9–dusk **Charges:** Entry fee **Tel:** 06 3996 7700 **Map:** p. 21, B2
The Colosseum's long queues can be skipped by buying a joint ticket at the Palatine Hill that allows entry to both sights on the same day, or to the Palatine the following day if you enter the Colosseum after 1.30.

The Colosseum, for many the definitive icon of Rome's brutal brilliance, was the largest amphitheatre of the ancient world, and its design was repeated all over Europe and North Africa. Despite centuries of pillaging and the earthquakes of 1231 and 1349, the building still retains its grandeur, and the northeast side remains fully intact. The amphitheatre was begun by Vespasian in AD 70 and completed by Titus ten years later. Its use for gladiatorial battles is well documented, but the arena also played host to animal hunts, or *venatii*, which featured elephants, rhinos and big cats brought from Africa, and it was even flooded in order to stage sea battles, or *naumachiae*. The name 'Colosseum' came from a 35m statue of Nero beside the building, which was modelled on the Colossus of Rhodes. The huge brick base of the colossus is the only part still standing.

The four storeys of the exterior wall support the complex interior. All 80 arches on the ground floor were numbered and served as entrances. The main entrance on the northeast was wider than the others, and opened into a stuccoed hall exclusively for the emperor. The building's total circumference is 545m.

The Colosseum could hold more than 50,000 spectators. The arena measures 83m by 48m and was surrounded by a high wall that protected the spectators from the animals. The emperor's podium was on top of this wall, and above this was the seating for the other spectators, in three tiers: the first for the equestrian classes, the middle for Roman citizens, and the third for the general public including women and slaves. The structures beneath the arena housed the scenery,

The Colosseum's interior, showing the structures beneath the arena

cages for animals, and other equipment that was hoisted up to provide backdrops to the hunts. Sand covered the floor to give combatants more grip and, of course, to absorb blood. The wooden floor was constructed in 2000.

The **Arch of Constantine** (*map p. 21, B2*) was erected in AD 315 and commemorates Constantine I's victory over rival emperor Maxentius in the battle at the Milvian Bridge just outside Rome three years earlier. The sculptures and reliefs have been recycled from various earlier monuments. The Constantine-era 'historical' reliefs under the monument's round panels depict the emperor's Italian campaign against Maxentius. At the western side is 'Departure from Milan'. On the southern side is the siege of a city, thought to be Verona, which was a pivotal moment of the campaign, as was the Battle of Milvian Bridge, which is featured on the same face, and shows the enemy troops drowning in the river Tiber.

San Pietro in Vincoli

Open: 7.30–12.30 & 3.30–6 **Charges:** Free entry **Map:** p. 21, B2
Highlights: Chains of St Peter; *Moses* statue by Michelangelo

This basilica was built in the mid-5th century to house one of the chains that apparently held St Peter while in prison close to the Forum. When the second chain was later brought to Rome from Constantinople the two are said to have miraculously joined together, and at once became one of the most revered relics in the city. They are displayed in the altar.

Michelangelo's astounding sculpture of **Moses** is at the end of the right-hand aisle. Pope Julius II ambitiously envisaged the statue as one of over 40 to adorn his funeral monument. Michelangelo was so careworn from working on the monument that he himself dubbed it 'the tragedy of a sepulchre' and ultimately accepted that his work on the tomb had been a failure; surviving contracts show the project progressively reduced in scale over the following 40 years. Julius II now rests inconspicuously in St Peter's.

Michelangelo's magnificent *Moses*, originally sculpted to form part of Pope Julius II's funeral monument

Moses, representing the Old Testament, was to have been placed level with a statue of St Paul portraying the New Testament. Instead we see Michelangelo's singular work as part of an incongruous group that was never intended. The horns on his head represent rays of light to signify his role as prophet. The beautiful figures of Leah and Rachel on either side—emblems of the active and contemplative life— are also by Michelangelo.

Domus Aurea (*open 9-7.45, closed Tues, free entry, Tel: 06 3996 7700*)
The 'Golden House' was built as a pleasure dome for Emperor Nero after
his other palace, on the Palatine Hill, was destroyed by fire in AD 64. Nero
commissioned the series of villas as a party complex where he could enjoy
the pleasures of the countryside inside the city boundaries. In fact, the site,
which also contained forests and an artificial lake on the subsequent site
of the Colosseum, made up one-third of Rome's area at that time.
Although not known for his winning personality—his reaction to the house
on completion was allegedly, 'Finally I am being housed like a human
being'—Nero took pomp and ceremony, and his status as an artist, very
seriously. The palace has a famous domed hall which made innovative use
of vaulting and a new type of Roman concrete made from local volcanic
ash and lime mixed with stones. The palace was also the earliest structure
to set mosaics in its ceilings, a technique that would become commonplace
throughout Christendom. The lake at the centre of the grounds was drained
to make way for the Colosseum after Nero's death, and the palace was
stripped of its ivory, marble and jewels and soon built over by his shame-
faced successors. The construction of the Baths of Titus over the palace
actually ensured its preservation, as did the Baths of Trajan and the
Temple of Venus and Rome. The palace was rediscovered in the 15th century, and Pinturicchio, Michelangelo and Raphael all crawled down to see
its frescoes. Their signatures now share wall space with later visitors such
as Casanova and the Marquis de Sade. **Map p. 21, B3**

Imperial Fora and Trajan's Column (*open 9.30–6.30, free entry*) The
Imperial Fora were first laid out by Julius Caesar (c. 34 BC) in order to
ease the overcrowding in the Roman Forum. Caesar and his successors
built temples to commemorate important events in Roman history. The
Fora were only rediscovered in the 1920s during excavations by Mussolini
to construct the massive Via dell'Impero (Via dei Fori Imperiali). Today,
only the Forum of Trajan and some of the Markets are open, the rest of
the ruins are visible from walkways and roads above. **Trajan's Column**
was built to commemorate the emperor's victories in Dacia (Romania) in

the second century AD. Some 2,500 figures make up the spiral bas-relief which depicts significant phases in the military campaign, and is still remarkably intact. **Map p. 21, A1**

First Lady of Rome

A discovery of a well preserved skeleton beneath Julius Caesar's Forum on a cold January morning in 2006 moved the city's culture head Gianni Borgna to declare that this would 'bring a whole new reading of the history of Rome', and uncovered yet another layer of ancient Roman history. Archaeologists uncovered the remains of a Latin woman who may have ruled Rome some two centuries before the previously accepted founding of the city in the 8th century BC by Romulus and Remus. She was buried with an amber necklace, bronze brooches and an ornament in her plaited hair. Such adornments—allied to the fact that she was not cremated—suggest that she was of high social rank: an excited Italian media dubbed her 'the Lady of the Forum' and 'Queen of the Latins'. The newly-uncovered necropolis beneath the Forum suggests that the woman was the wife of a tribal chief of the Latins, a farming and trading people who inhabited Rome in the 9th and 10th centuries BC. The development also proved that the city was inhabited by a sophisticated Bronze-age Latin culture long before Romulus.

The Palatine Hill and Circus Maximus (*open 9-dusk, entry fee*) The hill rising above the Forum is the site of the earliest settlement of Rome (legend tells that this is where the twins Romulus and Remus were found), and it later became a prestigious residential district with extravagant Imperial palaces being built on the slopes. Today, impressive ruins can still be seen and the area is one of the best places to view the extent of the Forum. The well-kept gardens are a particularly pleasant escape from the traffic of the city centre.

Circus Maximus is the oldest and largest of Rome's outdoor arenas, dating from around 600 BC. Athletic competitions, mock sea-battles and wild beast fights took place here, but the arena was primarily used for chariot racing. The bricks at the southern end are the original seating, and with a small leap of the imagination it is possible to visualise the races taking place around the flat basin, surrounded by stands on the sloping sides, which held up to 300,000 people. **Map p. 21, C1–D1**

San Clemente (*open 9–12.30 & 3–6, last entrance 12.10 and 5.40; Sun and holidays 12–6, entry fee to lower church*) This is one of the best preserved and oldest of Rome's medieval basilicas. Especially beautiful are the mosaics in the apse of the upper church, which date from the early 12th century, and the frescoes by Masolino da Panicale which cover the entire chapel of St Catherine. A staircase descends to the 1st-century

One of the beautiful mosaics which adorn the upper church of San Clemente

level where the remains of an ancient temple of Mithras can be seen, a popular cult in the Western Empire. **Map p. 21, C3**

Santi Cosma e Damiano (*open 9–12 & 4–6*) This church was converted in 527 and dedicated to the patron saints of doctors. It contains a wonderful 6th-7th century mosaic masterpiece, which depicts the two saints alongside Christ, St Peter and others. The decoration is particularly detailed and expressive and inspired other mosaics in the city. From a modern window at the west end it is possible to view the

Temple of Romulus in the Roman Forum which once served as an antechamber to the church. **Map p. 21, B2**

St John Lateran (*open 7–6; 7–7 in summer*) St John Lateran is the only cathedral in Rome and the official seat of the pope. All pontiffs were crowned here until 1870 and the church contains the tombs of six popes, including the last one not to be buried in St Peter's, Leo XIII. The church was built on the site of an ancient patrician family palace and was dedicated by Sylvester I in 324. It was the first Christian basilica to be built in Rome, and served as a model for all subsequent churches. After a history which included looting at the hands of the Vandals, and destruction by an earthquake in 896, the extensions and beautifications of Nicholas IV made it the great wonder of its age, admired by Dante among others. The basilica burned down twice in the 14th century, but Domenico Fontana, and later Borromini helped to rebuild it, the latter remodelling the 130-metre nave from 1646–49, including the niches now filled by titanic depictions of the twelve apostles, which were executed by a number of artists, from 1703 onwards. The ancient bronze doors of the Curia Julia in the Roman Forum were moved to the central portal in the 17th century. The late Baroque façade was completed by Alessandro Galilei in 1735. The square in front of the Lateran Palace contains the world's largest obelisk. Of red granite, it was erected in Thebes in the 15th century BC, and was brought to Rome by Constantius II in AD 357. **Map p. 21, D4**

Vittorio Emanuele II Monument (*open 10–4; 10–6 in summer; closed Mon, free entry*) This extravagant, incongruous tribute to Italian unity was begun by Giuseppe Sacconi in 1885, after he won the international tender to build it, and was inaugurated in 1911. Some 80m high, 'Mussolini's typewriter' changed the city forever, dwarfing the Capitoline Hill and causing widespread demolitions in the area. Its glaring white botticino marble is from Brescia, in northern Italy. **Map p. 21, A1**

eat

This is one of the more crowded areas of Rome with visitors flocking around the Colosseum and Forum; small cafés serving pizza and pasta dishes abound, but the best places to sit down and enjoy a good meal tend to be slightly further from the major visitor attractions. The long Via di San Giovanni in Laterano has places that cater to locals, and the smaller streets around San Pietro in Vincoli contain some pleasant hidden restaurants and cafés. For price categories, see p. 9.

1 €€ **La Tana dei Golosi**, *Via di San Giovanni in Laterano 220, Tel: 06 772 03202*. Part of the global Slow Food Network which was founded in 1989 to promote and encourage local and traditional gastronomy, La Tana dei Golosi uses fresh, organic produce to create innovative menus which focus on a different Italian region every few months. The delicious house dishes of *strozzapreti con limone e baccalà* ('priest strangler' pasta with lemon and salt cod) or the *costine d'abbacchio dorate con carciofi* (lamb ribs with artichoke) shouldn't be missed. The staff are particularly knowledgeable and the wine list extensive. **Map p. 21, C4**

2 € **Caffè Martini**, *Piazza del Colosseo 3a/b, Tel: 06 70 04 431*. Three cafés side-by-side on Piazza del Colosseo all have a close-up view of the Colosseum away from the crowds and with pavement seating in good weather. Caffè Martini is the best of the three.

There has been a restaurant here since the 19th century and the current owner, Vittorio, is often sitting inside totting up the bills. He has been running Caffè Martini since 1994. The two rooms inside have some original features and are pleasantly cool on a hot summer's day. Traditional (*a la romana*) thin-crust pizzas and large portions of pasta are served at reasonable prices. **Map p. 21, C3**

3 € **Hostaria Nerone**, *Via Terme di Tito 96, Tel: 06 481 7952*. On the doorstep of the Domus Aurea, this is a busy, family-run *trattoria* which has been operating since the 1930s and pleasing locals and visitors to the city ever since. The food is excellent and traditional with house favourites such as *frittata di carciofi* (a beautifully light Italian-style omelette with fresh artichoke) and *coda alla vaccinara* (oxtail stewed with celery) as well as a super *anti pasti* buffet with plenty of fresh vegetables. There are views of the

Just some of the vast selection of meats available to eat in Rome

Colosseum from the terrace. Reservations recommended. **Map p. 21, B2**

4 € Enoteca Cavour, *Via Cavour 313, Tel: 06 678 5496*. A traditional wine bar situated in the popular drinking district around Via Cavour, close to San Pietro in Vincoli and the Imperial Fora. The wine list is impressive, covering wine regions throughout Italy, and the cheese and meat snacks are said to be some of the best in Rome. Try the *torte rustiche*, a towering quiche, with a glass of crisp Frascati. **Map p. 21, A2**

5 € Vecchia Roma, *Via Leonina 10, Tel: 06 474 5887*. A bustling *trattoria* where it is advisable to 'go with the flow' and enjoy the atmosphere: you will rarely dine alone at Vecchia Roma. Good pizzas are served at very reasonable prices and the gnocchi with clam and mussel sauce is a speciality. If you arrive between sights then a *bruschetta* and a glass of the house wine is a perfect and inexpensive light lunch. **Map p. 21, A2**

shop

There are some good places to be discovered in this district, including some intriguing shops along Via di San Giovanni in Laterano (**map p. 21, C3–C4**). The Monti district (**map p. 21, A2–A3**) is the 'district of the hills' and has at its boundaries the Esquiline to the south and the Quirinal to the north. In Ancient Rome this area was the Subura, the rough part of town inhabited by prostitutes and thieves. Nowadays it preserves some old fashioned streets and has been transformed, with plenty of boutiques and gourmet shops.

At Via di San Giovanni in Laterano 58, **Stampe e Dipinti Antichi Arte Contemporanea** is a fantastic shop that sells antique lithographs and prints, and exudes old-school Roman class and charm. If you are planning to buy an art souvenir of your trip, then this is the place. The shop has links with several contemporary painters, but it is the limited-edition etchings and *aquafortes* of Rossini and Giovanni Battista Piranesi, who had a workshop on the Via del Corso, where this shop comes into its own. Piranesi, a great influence on Neoclassicism, was enchanted by Rome, and here you can purchase prints of his drawings of the ancient remains.

At no. 116 is **Passion**, which sells flowers, chocolates and other goods to ensure a romantic stay in the city that gave birth to the word.

Suzuganaru Uomo, at no. 204 is a mod-style clothing store which began selling to Anglophile locals and tourists alike four years ago. Owner Fabio says his mission is to provide 'something English, something Italian', and stocks a large selection from the Lambretta label, an English company with an Italian name, which burst onto the scene in 1997. In fact, the mod phenomenon is a rare example of British culture repackaging, something that it borrowed from Italy in the first place, as mopeds and loafers were staples of any self-respecting mod, and anyone around in the 1960s will associate the Lambretta scooter with this Italian-influenced style. This place specialises in retro shirts and coats, served with a friendly attitude.

Studio242, a framing house at no. 242, is owned by Massimo Musti, who followed his father into the trade 20 years ago. You can use this shop for a high-quality bespoke frame for your recently-purchased painting. Musti is also a restorer and puppet-maker.

In the Monti district the parallel streets of Vicolo dei Serpenti and Via del Boschetto have the most interesting selection of shops. **Spazio Artigiano**, at Vicolo dei Serpenti 13, specialises in luxurious, handmade goods from all over Italy. Ceramics from Sicily and beautifully coloured glassware are elegantly displayed. The owner, Christina Venezia, also creates her own fabrics on a loom in her studio: shawls, throws and cushion covers in natural materials such as linen, alpaca wool or silk. This is definitely a stop-off for that special gift to take home.

Il Giardino del Te, at Via del Boschetto 3, has a wonderful range of tea for those who loved

Babington's English Tea Room (*see p. 91*) but can't afford to drink there every day. At Giardino del Te you can't drink the tea on the premises but you can search through the shelves of Nilgiri, Pekoe, Sikkim, Snow Dragon, Yin Zhen and Gunpowder leaves for your special brew at home. In true Italian style, this teashop also sells a selection of coffee.

If you didn't bring the right wardrobe on holiday with you or you feel the need to splash out on a custom-made outfit then **Tina Sondergaard** at Via del Boschetto 1d is the place to visit. She is known for her unusual fabrics and retro-style and can provide anything from wool coats to evening dresses to casual suits.

Souvenir replicas of classical artwork for sale outside the Colosseum

THE TREVI DISTRICT

introduction

Countless visitors are drawn to the magnetic Trevi fountain to experience the atmosphere and throw their coins into the waters to ensure a return visit to Rome, and it is difficult to be disappointed by this Italian cliché. However, without having to venture too far it is also possible to see famous artworks of the Baroque era, monuments of Rome's ancient past, as well as relics of early Christianity here in the heart of the city.

The lively Via del Corso is downtown Rome's most ancient road, and is the location for two wonderful private art collections: the Palazzo Doria-Pamphilj which displays masterpieces by Velázquez and Titian, amongst others, in a sumptuous palace that has changed little throughout the last four centuries; and the Galleria Colonna with its antique sculpture and luxurious royal apartments.

The architectural greats, Borromini, Bernini and Maderno designed another palazzo in this area, Palazzo Barberini, home to superb works by Holbein, Caravaggio and Raphael, as well as the greatest ceiling fresco of the Baroque era. Close by you can glimpse into the bathing culture of the ancient Romans at the Baths of Diocletian.

The church of Santa Maria della Vittoria contains the *Ecstasy of St Teresa*, which the sculptor Gian Lorenzo Bernini considered his best work, and Santa Maria Maggiore has chapels commissioned by the illustrious Sforza and Borghese families.

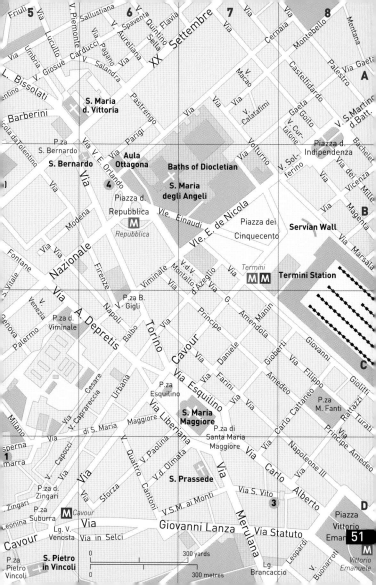

Trevi Fountain

The enchanting Trevi Fountain (*map p. 50, B2*) epitomises Rome's exuberant atmosphere, and multitudes of tourists gather here every day of the year. The gentle roar of rushing water adds to the cheery, chattering ambience around the small square. The fountain itself is a late Baroque design with a figure of Neptune as its centrepiece, flanked by statues symbolising health and abundance. Two giant tritons, one blowing a conch, appear to drive the god of the sea's horse-drawn chariot through the water, towards tourists throwing coins and taking photos at one of Rome's emblematic locations.

The fountain's name may come from *tre vie*, which refers to the three roads that once converged here. In 1732 Clement XII awarded the commission to replace the original 15th-century fountain to the little-known Roman architect and poet Niccolò Salvi. His ingenious design uses the entire Neoclassical façade of Palazzo Poli (1730) as a backdrop. The figures glide over stone expertly sculpted to resemble real rocks, a very difficult effect to achieve successfully. The fountain was completed after Salvi's death in 1762. Some 3,000 euros are collected from the Trevi each night—throw a coin in, they say, and you will return to Rome—and the money supports a supermarket providing food for disadvantaged families in the city.

Santa Maria Maggiore

Open: 7–7 **Charges:** Free entry **Map:** p. 51, C7
Highlights: Roman mosaic cycle; Bernini family tomb; Sistina, Borghese and Sforza chapels

Santa Maria Maggiore contains artistic treasures from many different eras. It is an ancient basilica (one of Rome's four major basilicas) and the only one that retains its 5th-century plan. It contains beautiful mosaics, elaborate tombs and sumptuous chapels from the 16th and 17th centuries, commissioned by some of the most powerful popes. The bell-tower is the highest in Rome.

Santa Maria Maggiore

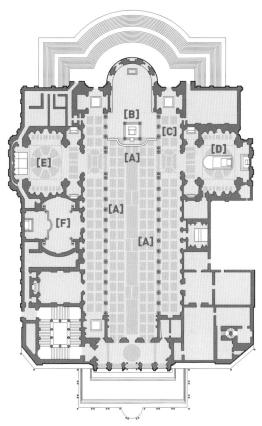

[A] Mosaics
[B] Statue of Pius IX
[C] Bernini Tomb

[D] Sistina Chapel
[E] Borghese Chapel
[F] Sforza Chapel

The church has a fascinating, if fanciful, legend from the 13th century attached to its origins. It tells the story of the Virgin appearing to Pope Liberius and to John, a patrician of Rome, on 5th August 358, telling them to build a church on the Esquiline Hill. A patch of snow the next morning would show them the exact spot on which to erect the church. When the miracle duly occurred (this was the middle of summer), Liberius drew up the plans and John financed the church from his own pocket. As a result the original name of the basilica was Santa Maria della Neve (of the Snow). The pope still says Mass here on 5th August.

The interior

Many of the architectural and sculptural works inside the church are by the four artists who also worked on the exterior: the 16th-century contemporaries Domenico Fontana and Flaminio Ponzio; Carlo Rainaldi, the principal architect at work in Rome at the end of the 17th century; and Ferdinando Fuga. King Ferdinand of Aragon and his wife Isabella, Queen of Castile, presented the church's extravagant coffered ceiling to the notorious Borgia pope, Alexander VI (who was also Spanish). Highlights are are given below, and marked on the plan on p. 53.

[A] **Mosaics:** Beneath the windows along the nave, and above the triumphal arch, are mosaics made from 432–40; the most important Roman mosaic cycle of that time. On the left are scenes from the life of Abraham, Jacob and Isaac; on the right are scenes from the life of Moses and Joshua, and over the triumphal arch are scenes from the early life of Christ. The mosaic in the apse (1288–94) depicts the Coronation of the Virgin. Underneath, between the windows, are more mosaics depicting the life of the Virgin, notably, in the centre, the Assumption. Older still are the marble columns supporting the nave, which either come from the original basilica built on this site, or from an ancient Roman building.

[B] **Statue of Pius IX:** Below the main altar is the *confessio*, containing a colossal kneeling statue of Pius IX, the arch-conservative pope who introduced the doctrine of Papal Infallibility in 1870. In the same year he became the last Pope to wield temporal power when Italian troops took the city as the capital of the Kingdom of Italy.

[C] Bernini family tomb: By the two sanctuary steps is the simple pavement tomb of the Bernini family, a surprisingly unassuming resting place for the great Baroque sculptor and architect Gian Lorenzo.

[D] Sistina Chapel: This is a work by Domenico Fontana (1585), the extraordinary opulence of which might be explained by the humble origins of the former swineherd who commissioned it, Sixtus V. It is decorated with statues, stuccoes, and Mannerist frescoes around Sixtus V's tomb, and that of St Pius V on the left.

[E] Borghese Chapel: This was erected for Paul V by Flaminio Ponzio in 1611 as the pope's burial chamber. A church within a church, the frescoes by Caravaggio's teacher Cavaliere d'Arpino are considered his masterpiece. To one side of the pope's tomb is that of Clement VIII, who went down in history as the pope who sent Beatrice Cenci (*see p. 62*) to her death.

[F] Sforza Chapel: This beautiful chapel, only recently restored, was erected by Giacomo della Porta to a design by Michelangelo.

Galleria Doria Pamphilj

Open: 7.30–12.30 & 3.30–7, closed Thur pm **Charges:** Entry fee
Tel: 06 679 7323 **Map:** p. 50, C2
Highlights: *Portrait of Innocent X* by Velázquez; *The Rest on the Flight into Egypt* and *Penitent Magdalene* by Caravaggio

The palazzo has been the home of the Doria Pamphilj family—famous Roman patricians—since the 17th century. The Pamphilj pope, Innocent X, started the collection in 1651 and Prince Andrea Doria IV added his inheritance in 1760 to form the arrangement that is seen today. Perhaps the most interesting aspect of the collection is the very same thing that makes it initially off-putting to a contemporary visitor: the works here have been painstakingly arranged to reflect late Baroque tastes: every possible inch of wall space is covered. The best approach is to dispel any thoughts of your grandmother's sitting room, and stroll around the rooms, as the members of the family that owns it have done for centuries—this remains one of the few Roman *palazzi* still inhabited by the descendants of those who originally built it—and immerse yourself in the opulence of the Baroque era. A selection of the most interesting rooms is detailed below.

[A] First Gallery: On the left are a number of works by Annibale Carracci, who came to work in Rome in 1595 and gave a new slant to Michelangelo's fresco techniques. His classically composed and measured *Flight into Egypt* is characteristic of this influential artist, who now lies in the Pantheon, near Raphael, his greatest inspiration. Carracci's work greatly affected the French painter Claude Lorrain who worked in Rome all his life and is represented here with numerous typically lyrical landscapes, including *Mercury stealing the Oxen of Apollo*. On the opposite wall is a satirical genre scene entitled *The Userers* by the Netherlandish painter Quinten Massys, who was born in 1465, and whose works frequently pass judgement on his materialistic contemporaries.

[B] Hall of Mirrors: Resplendent with gilded mirrors, this is the most attractive wing of the Palazzo. The Cabinet is home to the superb *Portrait of Innocent X (see p. 58)*, the most famous member of the Pamphilj family, which was commissioned by the pope himself in 1650 from Diego Velázquez, and painted during the artist's second stay in Rome

The ornate Hall of Mirrors at the Galleria Doria Pamphilj

Galleria Doria Pamphilj

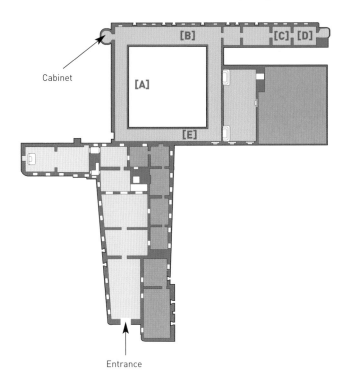

Cabinet

[B]

[C] [D]

[A]

[E]

Entrance

[A] First Gallery

[B] Hall of Mirrors

[C] Seventeenth-century Gallery

[D] Sixteenth-century Gallery

[E] Fourth Gallery

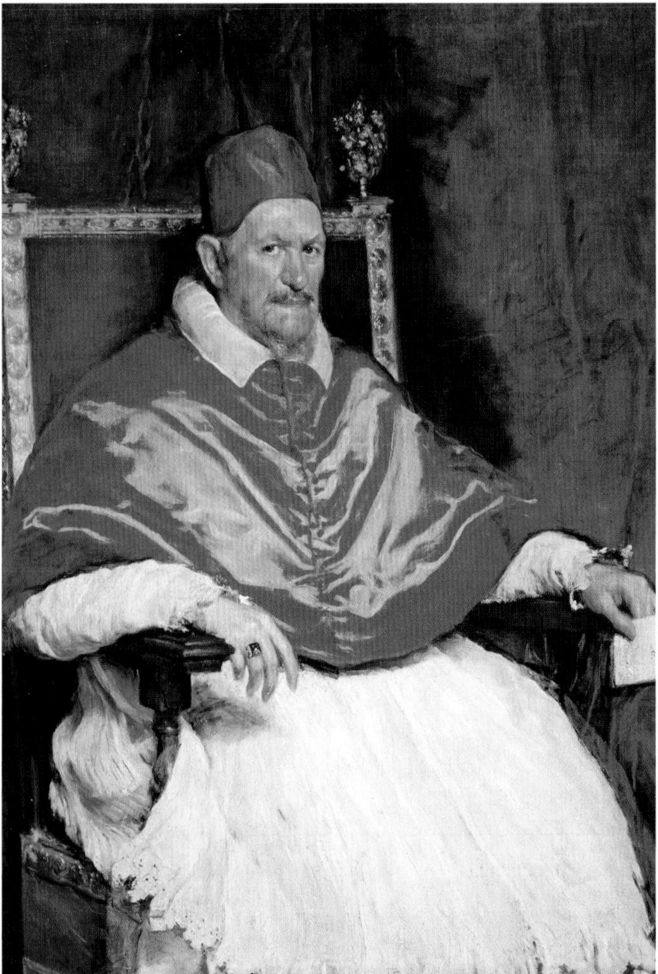

(he had previously lived in Italy for 18 months some years after becoming the leading artist at the court of Philip IV of Spain, aged just 24). The pointed realism evident in much of his work can be seen here in the severe features of the controversial but politically astute pontiff. Velázquez influenced the realist and impressionist painters of the 19th century, and his impact reverberates throughout the art world to this day. Beside Velázquez's painting is a bust of Innocent X by Bernini.

[C] Seventeenth-century gallery: The room contains two early masterpieces by Caravaggio, including his first large-scale work, *The Rest on the Flight into Egypt*, a tender composition with fine naturalistic details and a surprising serenity. The scene is dominated by the luminous figure of a young angel lulling the infant Jesus to sleep with a violin, in a rare moment of peace during the Holy family's flight from King Herod. The *Penitent Magdalene*, also known as Mary Magdalene, shows a desolate figure of Mary in a bare room, her jewels discarded at her feet and her trademark jar of oil beside her, and show her in transition from a life of lavishness towards a more simple existence. Caravaggio used the same model—a courtesan named Anna Bianchini—for the Madonna in the painting it hangs beside. The work demonstrates Caravaggio's facility for portraying inner conflict in a subject while making its representation sumptuous. Mary's clothing is contemporary to the era in which both works were executed (c. 1597).

[D] Sixteenth-century gallery: This room houses two sublime works: a double portrait of unidentified noblemen by Raphael, and Titian's *Salome with the Head of St John the Baptist*.

[E] Fourth gallery: The *Young St John the Baptist* by Caravaggio is a replica of the painting in the Vatican Picture Gallery (see p. 136). Also here are three works by Jan Brueghel the Elder, including the faded but captivating *Earthly Paradise*. The Saletta degli Specchi contains no fewer than seven paintings by the same artist, but is only sporadically open.

Detail from *Portrait of Innocent X*, by Diego Velázquez, in the Hall of Mirrors

Palazzo Barberini

Open: 9–7, closed Mon **Charges:** Entry fee **Entrance:** Via delle
Quattro Fontane. Wheelchair access to lift through small door to
the right of the building **Tel:** 06 482 4184 **Map:** 50, B4
Highlights: Salone ceiling fresco by Pietro da Cortona; *Judith with
the Head of Holofernes* by Caravaggio; and *Portrait of a Lady* or *'La
Fornarina'* by Raphael

Carlo Maderno began work on the palace for the Barberini pope
Urban VIII in 1624. Bernini completed the central block, and three
busts by him are displayed in the entrance. The monumental flight of
stairs was probably also designed by Bernini, while Borromini
designed the windows of the top storey, the building's other flight of
stairs, and the vastly influential three-sided courtyard. Pietro da
Cortona, who was also involved as architect, painted the astounding
ceiling fresco in the Salone, an allegory of Divine Providence (and of
Barberini power).

The Galleria Nazionale d'Arte Antica is one of Italy's most important art collections, with works by Caravaggio, Hans Holbein,
Nicholas Poussin, Raphael, Tintoretto and Tiepolo.

Left of the ticket office is the Salone, which contains Pietro da
Cortona's groundbreaking **ceiling fresco**, begun by the artist in 1633
and more or less completed in just three years. This High Baroque
masterpiece uses trompe l'oeil and varied lighting effects to take the
viewer on a dizzying visual journey of celestial figures soaring across
an illusionist architectural backdrop. The centre of the ceiling opens
up to the sky, where Divine Providence commands Faith, Hope and
Charity to crown three honeybees—the Barberini family's heraldic
arms—with the laurel leaf of Immortality. Towards the window the
Roman goddess of wisdom, Minerva, is depicted battling against
giants who are trying to break into heaven, representing the triumph
of intellect over brute force. In fact the whole fresco is allegorical,

Raphael's portrait of 'La Fornarina', thought to be his mistress, Margherita Luti

and was partly commissioned to portray Barberini's election to the pontificate as divine providence, and thus counter rumours circulating in Rome that the voting had been rigged.

The room, replete with comfy sofas and comprehensive information sheets, offers a relaxed setting for the visitor to sit back and take in a brace of dramatic Caravaggio paintings: *Narcissus*, and *Judith with the Head of Holofernes*. Nowadays, most experts generally attribute the *Narcissus* to Caravaggio (1598–99), not only due to the discovery of a 1645 export licence, but also the high level of inventiveness—notice the playing card composition, framing the subject's knee in the centre—as well as its stylistic similarity to his other works.

To the left hangs the shockingly violent **Judith with the Head of Holofernes**, which depicts the biblical heroine beheading her enemy, having first made him drunk. It captures the moment in which a man's life is ending: Holofernes has the rolling eyes of the departed, but a twisting, animated torso. Judith startles the viewer from the right, the opposite direction to the way a painting is read. The red curtain crowns this highly dramatic scene.

Past the ticket desk, in the first room on the left of the gallery's other wing is Raphael's *Portrait of a Lady*, which became known as '*La Fornarina*' (*see illustration on p. 61*) when the sitter was identified as Margherita Luti, the daughter of a Sienese baker (*fornaio*), and allegedly Raphael's mistress. Another *Portrait of a Lady*, in this case by Guido Reni, is thought to be a painting of Beatrice Cenci, who was executed at the age of 22, in 1599, for hiring assassins to kill her violent and abusive father. Although Beatrice never confessed to the murder, even when tortured, she was beheaded. Her story caught the imagination of the Romantics and inspired Percy Bysshe Shelley's celebrated verse drama *The Cenci*. The tragic heroine was also included in works by Charles Dickens, Stendhal and Nathaniel Hawthorne. The spiral staircase by Borromini leads up to nine rooms resplendent with Rococo decorations (1750-70), where the family resided until 1960.

in the area

Santa Prassede (*open 7–12 & 4–6.30, free entry*). Santa Prassede is famed for its mosaics. The building is dedicated to Praxedes, daughter of St Pudens, who is traditionally said to have been St Paul's first convert in Rome. To the left of the entrance is a little jewel box, the Chapel of St Zeno, built by St Paschal as a mausoleum for his mother, Theodora, from 817-24. This exquisite chapel, perfectly preserved, is the most important work of its time to have survived intact in Rome, and the only chapel in the city entirely covered with mosaics. They betray a distinct Byzantine influence, and the portrayal of animals demonstrates how pantheistic and pagan symbolism was amalgamated with Christian iconography.

The glittering mosaics in the vaulted interior are truly sublime. On the ceiling Christ is holding a scroll, surrounded by four angels (portraying Him as the victor over death). **Map p. 51, D7**

One of the mosaics in Santa Prassede, portraying Christ as victor over death

Galleria Colonna (*open Sat only 9–1, closed Aug, Tel: 06 678 4350, entrance at Via della Pilotta 17*). Like the Galleria Doria Pamphilj, this is a private collection housed in a sumptuous palazzo which is decorated with frescoes, mirrors and antique sculpture, all beautifully kept. The apartment of the Principessa Isabelle can be seen by appointment. Lorenzo Onofrio Colonna began the collection of paintings with guidance from the painter Carlo Maratta in the mid-17th century. Wonderful pieces of the collection include works by Jacopo Tintoretto, Annibale Carracci and Paolo Veronese. On the steps to the Great Hall is a cannonball which fell here during the Siege of Rome in 1849 and has never been removed. **Map p. 50, C2**

Santa Maria della Vittoria (*open 7–12 & 4–7*). This church, with its well-proportioned interior by Carlo Maderno, is considered one of the most complete examples of Baroque decoration in Rome, rich in colour and glowing with marbles. The church is most famous for the Cornaro Chapel by Bernini (the fourth on the left side), a splendid architectural achievement, using the shallow space to great effect (c. 1647–50). Over the altar is his famous marble group, the *Ecstasy of St Teresa*, showing the saint in an almost erotic swoon before an angel beneath golden rays of celestial light (also lit, ingeniously, from a hidden side window). Teresa of Avila, a Carmelite nun, left a description of her ecstasy in which an angel of the Lord pierced her heart, and Bernini, a devout Catholic, vividly portrays the divine moment in his work here. Scholars usually agree with Bernini himself in considering the chapel and this sculpture his best work. At the sides are expressive portraits by pupils and followers of Bernini of the Venetian family of Bernini's patron, Cardinal Federigo Cornaro. The last, half-hidden figure on the left is said to be a portrait of Bernini himself. **Map p. 51, A6**

The Corso. The long, straight Via del Corso represents the urban section of the Via Flaminia (221 BC), which was the main road to northern Italy in the days of ancient Rome. At that time it was called the Via Lata ('broad way') because of its exceptional width, compared to the other roads in the ancient city. Today, with its grand palaces, Baroque churches, elegant shops and bustling atmosphere, it is one of the streets which best characterises the city. Off the Corso (at Via del Caravita) is the Rococo **Piazza di Sant'Ignazio**, a theatrical masterpiece by Filippo Raguzzini (1728). The buildings have curving façades that fit into a careful decorative scheme in relation to the streets between them. The effect is that of a stage-set rather than a piazza. The main building is a church dedicated to the

A detail from the Column of Marcus Aurelius in Piazza Colonna

founder of the Jesuits, Ignatius Loyola, with a wonderful trompe l'oeil ceiling. **Piazza Colonna** was for centuries considered the centre of the city, and remains important today as the official residence of the Prime Minister. It takes its name from the majestic **Column of Marcus Aurelius**, or Colonna Antonina (AD 180–196). The column was built in honour of Marcus Aurelius' victories over barbarian tribes. The style of the carving anticipates the sustained period of crisis in the Roman Empire, which worsened after his death in AD 180. The heads are disproportionately large and deeply carved so the facial expressions can be viewed clearly. Many of the scenes depict the reality of the horrors of war, whilst the emperor is portrayed head-on, symbolic and god-like, emphasising and justifying his authority. On the Corso, in a wide piazza, is the church of **San Silvestro in Capite** (*open 7–12.30*). The *capite* refers to a relic of the head of St John the Baptist that is preserved here. **Map p. 50, A1–C2**
Baths of Diocletian (*open 9–7.45, closed Mon, Tel: 06 3996 7700, entrance through garden in front of the railway station*). The splendid vaulted rooms of the Baths of Diocletian (*Terme di Diocleziano*) provided a superb setting for over 3,000 bathers at one time. Begun in 299, the baths were completed in less than eight years by Diocletian and Maximian, and were the largest of all the ancient Roman baths, covering an area of roughly 380m by 370m. The *calidarium*, which survived into the late 17th century, occupied part of Piazza della Repubblica. The *tepidarium* and the huge central hall of the baths are now occupied by the church of Santa Maria degli Angeli (*see below*). The *frigidarium* was an open-air bath behind this hall. The **Octagonal Hall** or Aula Ottagona (*open 9–2, holidays 9–1, closed Mon, free entry*) which once connected the exercise areas with the *calidarium*, now displays statues and busts found at the baths. The church of **Santa Maria degli Angeli** (*open 7.30–12.30 &*

a/s/e Rome

4–6.30, free entry) was once the *tepidarium*, and the cavernous interior shows how vast these baths were. Most interesting, inside the church, is the Meridian line along the transept which was drawn in 1702 to test the accuracy of the new Gregorian calendar. The sun hits the line through a hole in the wall at around 12.15 each day (1.15 in summer). At the summer solstice (21st June) the sun hits the line at the point nearest the wall, while on 21st December it crosses the line at the furthest point. The sacristy door in the left transept leads to the remains of the *frigidarium*. **Map p. 51, B6**

Ancient Romans and their baths

Public bathing was extremely important in ancient Roman society. Far from being an elite pursuit, baths were affordable for most Roman citizens, and men and women from all levels of society considered the baths as the central venue of their social and recreational lives. Larger bath complexes were cities within cities, and also contained small theatres for poetry readings, libraries, shops, restaurants and sleeping quarters, in addition to the *calidarium* (hot water pool) *tepidarium* (warm water pool) and *frigidarium* (cold water pool), and perhaps a *laconium* (sauna) and *sudatorium* (sweat room).

Women and men originally bathed together, but after numerous scandals segregation was enforced from the 2nd century AD. Under Emperor Trajan the blueprint for a bathing complex was finally perfected, in which women would generally attend in the morning and men during the rest of the day.

A bather usually arrived with brushes, an oil flask (the poor used lentil flour instead), a dish for scooping water and a strigil (a curved piece of metal to scrape oil from the body), all of which were attached to a ring. After undressing, the bather would either take some exercise—often wrestling or a ball game—or go straight to be oiled and massaged, after which baths were taken.

Not all Romans were enamoured with bathing culture however, and the philosopher Seneca criticised the sweat being washed away by the waters as 'no longer coming from honest toil, but as the result of pummelling by attendants.'

eat

This area has some first-class restaurants close to Palazzo Barberini as well as special local *trattorie* which serve traditional Italian specialities. Some of the best *gelaterie* are here too, which make the perfect accompaniment for watching the crowds at the Trevi Fountain. For price categories, see p. 9.

RESTAURANTS

1 €€€ **La Carbonara**, *Via Panisperna 214, Tel: 06 482 5176.* Situated in one of the new chic areas of Rome, away from the crowds and close to Santa Maria Maggiore and the popular Via Cavour, La Carbonara serves Roman fare with a Jewish influence. A testament to its culinary prowess, by 8.30pm the restaurant is usually full with Roman diners enjoying the trademark fresh pasta *alla Carbonara*. This restaurant shouldn't be confused with the slightly more expensive and not so friendly establishment of the same name on Campo dei Fiori. Closed Sun. **Map p. 51, D5**

2 €€€ **Le Colline Emiliane**, *Via degli Avignonesi 22, Tel: 06 481 7538.* ■ On a quiet side street very close to Palazzo Barberini, this is a small, family-run restaurant which has garnered an excellent reputation for classic cuisine from the northern Italian region of Emilia-Romagna. The *tagliatelle alla bolognese* is mouthwatering, as is the *ravioli di zucca* (pumpkin ravioli). However, Le Colline Emiliane offers much more besides pasta and their meat dishes are also excellent. Try the delicious rolled pork stuffed with ham and cheese. Closed Sun and Aug. **Map p. 50, B4**

3 €€€ **Trattoria Monti**, *Via San Vito 13, Tel: 06 446 6573.* Trattoria Monti is one of the old-style restaurants that make you feel as though you have discovered a little bit of hidden Rome. Originally hailing from the Marche, on the east coast of Italy, the Camerucci family ensure that the fish, meat and game from that region feature heavily on the menu. Ask for the *tagliatelle alla papera*, perhaps with duck ragout. However, it is the *tortini* which most people come to Trattoria Monti for—exquisite savoury custard pies, the best are made with Parmesan cheese. **Map p. 51, D7**

CAFÉS & WINE BARS

④ Dagnino, *Galleria Esedra, Via V. Emanuele Orlando 75*. Dagnino specialises in Sicilian cuisine but somehow it might be the most Roman place you will wander into during your whole trip. The curt yet charismatic service from waiters in bow ties and white jackets and queuing alongside locals for one of the four or five daily specials, makes this place a memorable Roman experience. Lunching workers come to this 50s art deco eatery for such specialities as *rancine* (little oranges), deep-fried balls of rice with a meat, fish or vegetable filling served with tomato sauce. However, this restaurant-cum-confectioners is most notable for its dizzying display of traditional delicacies native to Sicily such as the *cannoli di carnevale* (a small cream-filled cake) and the *cassata di pasqua* (a fruitcake with dried, sugared fruits). **Map p. 51, B6**

⑤ Gelateria della Palma, *Via Lavatore 44-47*. This branch of the Roman *gelato* chain is just a coin's toss from the Trevi fountain, and sells a range of delicious flavours such as tiramisu, peach, and chocolate with candied orange peel. There are several great *gelaterie* around the square, and this establishment, which is a couple of doors down the street to the right if you are facing the fountain, is one of the best. **Map p. 50, B2**

⑥ Gelato di San Crispino, *Via della Panetteria 42*. San Crispino is a little less showy than some of the other ice-cream shops in the city— the ice-creams are kept well hidden in large, stainless steel tubs. However, this is an excellent branch of an all-natural ice cream company (the original shop is at Via Acaia). The honey speciality is based on a Buontalenti recipe from the 16th century and is delicious. Situated in a quiet street near to the Trevi Fountain, there is often a queue. **Map p. 50, B3**

⑦ Vineria Il Chianti, *Via del Lavatore 81, Tel: 06 679 2470*. A real gem just steps away from the Trevi Fountain. A wine bar with friendly staff, an extensive but unpretentious wine list, good value food (the wild boar and steaks are certainly above average) and a courtyard for *al fresco* dining right in the heart of the city. There isn't much more you could ask for. **Map p. 50, B3**

⑧ Vitti, *Piazza Lorenzo in Lucina 33*. Vitti is a simple, pleasant bar on the corner of the pretty Piazza Lorenzo in Lucina. The best thing about the bar is sitting outside on the narrow pavement and watching the stream of passers-by while you nurse a *caffè lungo* or an ice-cold bottle of Nastro Azzurro. Further down the street at no. 29 is **Ciampini** with a larger area to sit outside. **Map p. 50, A1**

shop

Anglo American Bookstore, *Via della Vite 102, Tel: 06 679 5222*. This well-stocked bookshop is a good place to visit if you have run out of reading material and want to see yourself through till the airport, or to find the perfect book to while away a couple of hours in a café you spotted earlier. Running since 1953 the shop is well-placed to offer an enviable array of books on any subject from archaeology to religion to cookery as well as a large fiction section. They also have another premises at no. 27 which has a technical and scientific section if you're feeling particularly brainy. Closed Sat pm and Sun. **Map p. 50, A2**

La Feltrinelli Libri e Musica, *Piazza Colonna 31/35 (Galleria Alberto Sordi), Tel: 06 6975 5001*. This shop is part of an excellent chain of book and music shops across the city, this branch is inside the Galleria Alberto Sordi (named after one of Italy's best-loved comedy actors who was born in Rome and on his eightieth birthday, in 2000, was made honorary mayor of the city for the day). La Feltrinelli has everything you would expect from a modern book and music store—shelves and shelves of the latest bestsellers, hi-tech headphones for listening to the latest albums, helpful staff and extra comfy sofas, with the added bonus of being inside a stylish shopping arcade. **Map p. 50, B1**

Saby's Bean, *Via del Tritone 123, Tel: 06 4782 3540*. A staggering array of Italian delicacies makes Saby's Bean the ideal one-stop shop for picnic ingredients en route to the Villa Borghese gardens, or for gourmets planning to relive their trip's culinary highlights at home. The staff here are extremely friendly, and will let you sample any of the exclusively Italian stock before you buy. Particularly recommended is the coffee: La Regina dei Caffè is a typically Roman coffee brand made from Arabica beans and worth the weight in your suitcase; and the top-quality Mussini brand of balsamic vinegar. The many herbs on sale will lend an Italian flavour to any dish that you are planning to rustle up back home, and the fresh pasta is as good as any you will find in the whole city. Saby's also sells fantastic fresh salad bowls to take away, and don't miss the exquisite, handmade Perla chocolates. **Map p. 50, B3**

FASHION

Via Frattina (**map p. 50, A1–A2**), is still somehow the little sister of the über-elegant Vias Condotti and Borgognona which it sits beside (*see p. 92–94*), and although it is still the venue for high-end clothing, most of the shops here are a little bit more affordable.

Gerard Darel, at no. 60 (*Tel: 06 678 1337*), is a French design house which produces feminine dresses with floral patterns, alongside chunky knitted cardigans, huge sunglasses and dressy handbags. It also has a natty line in ballet shoes and necklaces.

At no. 22 is **Max Mara** (*Tel: 06 679 3638; see box opposite*), a mainstay of Italian fashion, and still produces great clothes for women, whether they be cocktail dresses, one piece swimsuits or dress suits, all of which are on sale here.

Elena Miro, towards Piazza di Spagna, at no. 11 (*Tel: 06 678 4367*), sells clothes for ladies who want to look like Audrey Hepburn, without having to endure the strict diet of a Hollywood icon. Flattering cuts and primary colours are the order of the day here, as are lace-up shoes and variations on the classic Chanel suit. The shop also sells embroidered silk dresses, leather gloves, woollen snoods, scarves and elegant trenchcoats.

At no. 44 is **Patrizia Pepe** (*Tel: 06 678 1851*), which sells elegant, loose-fitting dresses, leather jackets and shoes and puts an emphasis on minimalism and comfort. This fashion house was formed in the early 90s and is currently trying to break into the big league. It also has a new men's clothing line that leans slightly towards 70s and 80s retro.

Sisley, at 19/19a (*Tel: 06 699 41787*), may be owned by the caring and sharing Benetton, but these designs utilise vampy clingy shimmering silks to create dresses to kill, and shiny stilletos which could have a similar effect. As for the men, any aspiring dandies can stock up on their cravates, quarter length coats and Dickensian hats here. Thankfully, they tone it down slightly for the junior range.

Sorelle Fontana, *Via Della Fontanella di Borghese 67, Tel: 06 687 9124*, is an Italian icon (*see box on following page*), and still sells classically elegant clothes and accessories here today. Map p. 50, A1

Max Mara

Achille Maramotti, a daring entrepreneur, built the fashion giant Max Mara on his vision of a brand that epitomised Italian craftsmanship, rather than the designer's personality. He quickly became one of post-war Italy's richest men, from his ready-to-wear concept, and a major collector of contemporary art in the process. The firm now has over 20 labels, and some 1,700 shops worldwide.

Maramotti started Max Mara in 1951. In the company's infancy, Maramotti persuaded fabric shops to include Max Mara clothing in their window displays. He hired designers like Karl Lagerfeld and later Franco Moschino to work for him anonymously, to ensure a sense of upmarket chic. In addition, he gave his new company a recognisable brand that combined the family name with the moniker of Count Max, a dandy who blew his fortune in bars throughout Europe.

He had a longterm business plan, and what his son Luigi, who took the reins of the empire in 1989, called a 'sense of the future', as well as a healthy disdain for celebrity. Maramotti famously said that he would prefer to see a photograph of Isabella Rossellini at Milan airport in a Max Mara coat she had bought for herself, rather than one of her at the Oscars in a dress they had paid her to wear.

He was 25 when he acquired his first important work of contemporary art, by the Italian abstract expressionist Alberto Burri. Later his collection of avant-garde canvases included works by artists Giorgio Morandi, Giorgio de Chirico and Alberto Savinio and has grown to be one of the biggest Renaissance and modern art collections in the world.

Practical to the end, fashion editors who visited him found that the logo'ed goody bag they were presented with on departure contained a large chunk of Parmesan cheese from the family herd. He died in 2005, aged 78.

Sorelle Fontana: a rags to riches fairytale

The story of Rome's oldest fashion house, Sorelle Fontana, is one of the industry's most alluring tales.

Three sisters, Zoe, Micol and Giovanna Fontana were tutored in dressmaking by their mother who had inherited an atelier in 1907. When the eldest sister Zoe was joined by her sisters and her mother in Rome—legend has it that she would have taken a Milan-bound train if one had arrived first—that this supremely united family began their rise.

At this time, the late 1930s, Paris was the centre of fashion while Rome was not even on the seasonal circuit, but the sisters challenged this monopoly and before long their designs with full skirts and clinging bust-lines gained popularity amongst the Italian aristocracy. The sisters felt that their less formal and sexier styles might also appeal to the Americans, and gained instant success after visiting the United States in 1951.

With their revolutionary and uniquely Italian conceptions, the sisters made dresses featuring images by contemporary artists, and also designed uniforms for Alitalia stewardesses, UN hostesses and bankworkers. Their most daring garments included a cassock-dress for Ava Gardner based on a Catholic priest's robe, and the frock worn by Anita Ekberg as she frolicked in the Trevi Fountain in *La Dolce Vita*. Sorelle Fontana came to epitomise the decadent lifestyle of the new jet set and prominent clients included Princess Grace of Monaco, Jacqueline Kennedy, Ursula Andress, Joan Collins and Elizabeth Taylor.

In subsequent years, the sisters produced a line of prêt-á-porter designs and moved their shop to its current location in the mid-1960s. Zoe Fontana, who looked after the company's financial matters, died in 1979, while Giovanna died in 2004, aged 88. Their name lives on, however, and remains synonymous with glamour for present-day Hollywood stars and royalty alike.

SPANISH
STEPS

introduction

This stylish part of Rome combines the artistic treasures of Villa Borghese park with the city's most exclusive shopping street, Via Condotti.

The Spanish steps lead up from the bustling Piazza di Spagna, which has long been a meeting point for foreign visitors. The poet Keats lived and died here and is honoured with a museum.

The park of Villa Borghese plays host to the sumptuous Museo and Galleria Borghese, a 16th-century villa with a sublime collection of sculptures by Bernini and Canova, amongst many others, as well as six paintings by Caravaggio. Across the park is the Etruscan museum. It displays exhibits from the civilisation which had a profound influence on early Roman culture.

Piazza del Popolo, a wide and impressive square, contains Santa Maria del Popolo, with its masterpieces by Raphael, Bramante and the famed paintings of St Peter and St Paul by Caravaggio. Also in the area is a striking, modern architectural development; a hi-tech construction built to house an important artistic treasure of 1st-century BC Rome, the Ara Pacis, which will no doubt provoke debate for many years to come.

Piazza di Spagna

Map: p. 75, D2 **Highlights:** Fontana della Barcaccia by Bernini; Spanish Steps; Keats house

Piazza di Spagna has a long tradition of welcoming visitors, and is a wonderful place to take in the vibrant, youthful atmosphere of Rome. Locals and visitors alike often meet at the **Fontana della Barcaccia** (the old boat fountain, 1627), which sits at the bottom of the Spanish Steps, and is thought to be the work of Bernini. Though not amongst the city's most beautiful fountains, it perhaps has the most amiable atmosphere. Legend has it that its 'leaking boat' design was inspired by a ship that ran aground here after the Tiber flooded in 1598.

Many of the city's most elegant shopping streets lead off the square—Via Condotti and Via Borgognona (*see pp. 92–94*).

The **Spanish Steps** (*Scalinata della Trinità dei Monti*) were constructed in 1723–26 to connect the piazza with the church of Trinità dei Monti. The 137-step staircase is a masterpiece of 18th-century town planning. The stairs derive their name from their proximity to the official residence of the Spanish ambassador to the Vatican.

The poet John Keats spent his last months in the small pink house at the foot of the steps on the right. The **Keats-Shelley Memorial House** (*open Mon-Fri 9-1 & 3-6: Sat 11-2 & 3-6:*

Detail of the popular Fontana della Barcaccia in Piazza di Spagna

Water games in Piazza del Popolo

closed Sun; T: 06 678 4235) has exhibits on several of the English Romantic poets. The apartment of the great Metaphysical painter Giorgio de Chirico can also be visited, at no. 31 Piazza di Spagna (*open 1st Sun of month except Aug, or by appointment Tues–Sat 10–1; Tel: 06 679 6546*). The apartment was where de Chirico lived and worked from 1947–78, and each of the paintings exhibited here were chosen and hung by the artist himself.

PIAZZA DEL POPOLO

This gigantic square (*map p. 75, C1*) was built to provide an impressive entry into the city from the north, and combines the designs of Rome's two architectural titans, Michelangelo and Bernini. The outer face of the main entrance gate at the far end was built to a design by Michelangelo (1561); the inner face was designed by Bernini. The piazza was created in 1538 for Pope Paul III around the three straight

The vivid and theatrical realism of Caravaggio's *Crucifixion of St Peter* in Santa Maria del Popolo

roads which lead from it, and the pair of twin-domed churches were added in the 17th century. The piazza plays host to some lovely cafés and restaurants (*see pp. 89–91*).

Santa Maria del Popolo

Open: 7–12 & 4–7 **Charges:** Free entry **Map:** p. 75, C1
Highlights: *Crucifixion of St Peter* and *Conversion of St Paul* by Caravaggio; Chigi Chapel; *Habakkuk* statue by Bernini

Pope Paschal II financed a chapel on this site, dedicated to the Virgin, from Roman taxpayers' funds in 1099. Today it is one of the more peaceful churches in the city and has a pleasant atmosphere in which to appreciate its wealth of art.

Above the high altar is the *Madonna del Popolo*, a revered painting from the 14th century. The apse, with its shell design, is one of Donato Bramante's earliest works in Rome (1505), and was commissioned by Julius II (*there is a light on the left*). The frescoes, high up in the vault are the Umbrian artist Pinturicchio's best works in the church (1508–09).

The first chapel to the left of the choir accommodates a pair of Caravaggio masterpieces: the **Crucifixion of St Peter** and the **Conversion of St Paul** (1600–01). The former depicts St Peter nailed to a heavy cross. The focus is not so much on the saint, however, rather on the three executioners and their physical struggle to lift an aged man. In the *Conversion of St Paul*, once again it is not the saint who fixes our attention but rather the carthorse stepping over the supine figure of Saul, who has 'seen the light'. The realistic focus of the paintings was criticised at the time.

Raphael and Bernini played key roles in the creation of the octagonal **Chigi Chapel** (1513–16), in the aisle leading from the Caravaggio paintings. It was founded by the powerful banker—and Raphael's patron—Agostino Chigi (1465–1520). Here, Raphael fused painting, architecture, sculpture and mosaic to stunning effect. The mosaics in the dome were executed by a Venetian artist from cartoons by Raphael: God is surrounded by symbols of the seven planets then known, each guided by an angel. Work on the chapel ceased for over a century after the deaths of both Chigi and Raphael in 1520, and was completed by Bernini from 1652, after Cardinal Fabio Chigi (Alexander VII) asked him to add Baroque touches to the Renaissance church.

Next to the altar is Bernini's celebrated *Habakkuk* (right) showing his late style of elongated bodies and expressive gestures. The angel, pulling Habakkuk's hair, urges him to take food to Daniel caught in the lion's den. Bernini's *Daniel with the Lion* is by the entrance to the chapel.

The extraordinary pyramidal form of the tombs of Agostino Chigi and his brother Sigismondo are by the Tuscan sculptor Lorenzetto. The form of Raphael's original architectural scheme comes from ancient Roman models, though it was altered again by Bernini in the 17th century. Bernini added the marble inlaid figure of Death, with the Chigi coat of arms in the centre of the pavement.

The first and third chapels on the right side of the church contain more frescoes by Pinturicchio.

Museo & Galleria Borghese

Open: 9–7.30, closed Mon **Charges:** Entry fee **Tel:** 06 328101 **Map:** p. 75, B4

Highlights: *Pauline Borghese* by Canova; *David* and *Apollo and Daphne* by Bernini; *The Sick Bacchus* and *Madonna of the Palafrenieri* by Caravaggio

NB: *It is obligatory to book your visit in advance, the entry fee covers only a strictly enforced two-hour period in the museum (which start at 9, 11, 1, 3 and 5).*

Within the wonderful park of Villa Borghese is the former home of the Borghese family and now the Museo and Galleria Borghese. The Borghese pope Paul V, who is buried in Santa Maria Maggiore (*see pp. 52–55*), lent his architect, Flaminio Ponzio, to the project and construction began in 1608. Paul V also helped procure numerous works of art for his nephew Cardinal Scipione Borghese who went on to create the extensive collection that can be seen today. Cardinal Scipione was Bernini's first important patron and also owned no fewer than 12 paintings by Caravaggio, six of which can be seen in the gallery.

Museo & Galleria Borghese
(Ground floor: sculpture)

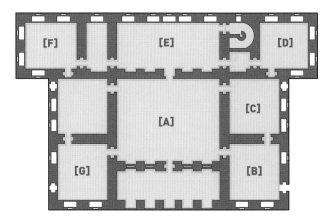

Ground floor and Sculpture Collection

[A] The Salone: This room is representative of the sumptuously decorated ground floor. Antique busts and sculptures are placed alongside 17th-century statues and the walls are covered with precious marbles and early reliefs. The ceilings are intricately frescoed while ancient Roman mosaics are set into the floors to great effect. The relief of Curtius is particularly arresting as it appears to leap down from high up on the wall, mirroring the myth surrounding the brave Roman citizen who, in 362 BC, plunged himself and his horse into a chasm to save Rome, following a declaration from a fortune-teller that Rome's greatest

Bernini's Baroque-style statue of *David*

set at its peculiar angle by Gian Lorenzo Bernini's father, Pietro.

[B] Room I: Antonio Canova's bold Neoclassical **sculpture of Pauline Borghese** is one of the sculptor's most well-known works. The partially nude depiction of Napoleon's equally daring favourite sibling, who married into the Borghese family, is provocative. It was justified at the time by the fact that she is depicted as Venus Victrix, in other words the goddess Venus who has just been chosen by Paris over her rivals Juno and Minerva as greatest of all the goddesses for her gift of love. She holds the golden apple awarded as her prize, in her hand. The statue's wooden base initially covered a mechanism to rotate the sculpture.

[C] Room II: Bernini made his self-portrait statue of ***David*** (see

treasure would have to be sacrificed. Curtius declared that there was no greater treasure than a brave citizen, and hurled himself headlong in. This 2nd-century Roman work was recrafted and

above) for Cardinal Scipione, from 1623–24, at the age of just 25. It depicts the subject with a furrowed brow while his straining body summons up the kinetic force necessary to kill Goliath. The work represents Bernini's Baroque style in the way that it endeavours to create dynamism from inflexible stone. Bernini was deeply influenced by Annibale Carracci, whose painting of *Samson in Prison* is also hung here.

Bernini (1598–1680)

Although Gian Lorenzo Bernini was Neopolitan by birth, his name is synonymous with Baroque sculpture and architecture in Rome, where he spent most of his working life, except for a brief spell in France working for Louis XIV in 1665. The child prodigy Gian Lorenzo began his career with his father Pietro— also a sculptor—and was commissioned to carve a bust of the Borghese pope Paul V by the pontiff in 1617. Soon after, the pope's nephew, Cardinal Scipione Borghese, commissioned Bernini's sculptures of *David*, and *Apollo and Daphne*, which can still be seen here in the Galleria Borghese. These sublime works ensured that Bernini was acknowledged as the most extravagantly talented artist of his generation.

The Barberini pope Urban VIII, who became the devout sculptor's main patron and close friend, brought him in to work on St Peter's. Artists also travelled to Rome to study under Bernini, and his busy workshop received numerous commissions thanks to his burgeoning status as Europe's most famous sculptor and architect.

After Urban VIII's death, Bernini was overlooked by the papal court for a short time, although Urban's successor, Innocent X, commissioned him to create his celebrated fountain in Piazza Navona (*see p. 101*). Bernini also worked for Alexander VII on a number of projects at St Peter's (*see p. 121*) and the Chigi Chapel in Santa Maria del Popolo (*see p. 79*). His incomparable buildings, fountains, sculptures and monuments draw visitors from all over the world.

[D] Room III: Bernini's *Apollo and Daphne* (1624) was also produced for Cardinal Scipione and is perhaps the sculptor's most famous work. It captures the transcendental moment from Ovid's *Metamorphoses* when Apollo finally reaches the nymph, with whom he has fallen in love, but she flees from him and is transformed into a laurel tree by the gods. A depiction of this difficult subject was unprecedented in sculpture. Apollo's face, hairstyle and sandals betray Bernini's admiration for the *Apollo Belvedere* (*see p. 136*). Daphne's hair flows with masterful delicacy, her fingers morph into leaf. Bernini designed this group to be viewed side-on, placed against a wall. However, nowadays there is the advantage of being able to view the stages of Daphne's transformation by walking around the statue.

[E] Room IV: The *Rape of Persephone* is the earliest of the three masterpieces Bernini made for the Borghese, and was designed to be seen from a single perspective. It portrays Pluto triumphant over Cerberus at the door of Hades, seizing Persephone in his arms as she struggles to free herself from his embrace. A masterful detail is Pluto's left hand sinking into Persephone's thigh.

[F] Room VI: The Aeneas and Anchises sculptural group was carved by a 20-year-old Bernini aided by his father. Details of the carving reveal Bernini's precocious talent. Also here is a late Bernini work representing Truth, planned as part of an uncompleted allegorical group entitled *Truth Unveiled by Time.*

[G] Room VIII: The six Caravaggio paintings here include *The Sick Bacchus* and *Boy with a Basket of Fruit*, both c. 1594. Caravaggio paints himself into the former, as he often did, and the latter is indicative of his naturalistic skill with a superb still life of a fruit basket. The *Madonna of the Palafrenieri* was commissioned for St Peter's but was rejected before being purchased by Cardinal Scipioni. *St Jerome*, dating from the same year, has a brilliant red cloak: the image is reduced to its essentials by Caravaggio's skilful use of light. The *Young St John the Baptist* is the volatile artist's last known work: Caravaggio sent it to Cardinal Scipione to seek a papal pardon for a murder he had committed and for permission to return to Rome, something which would not ultimately happen (*see p. 103*).

Museo & Galleria Borghese
(Upper floor: paintings)

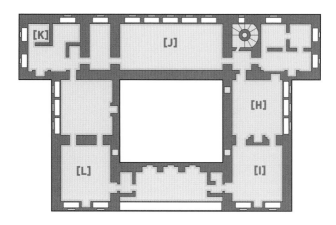

Upper floor and Gallery of Paintings

[H] **Room IX:** Two sublime Raphael paintings greet you on your arrival upstairs. The recently restored *Entombment* (1507) depicts Christ's body being carried to his tomb. It is known that Raphael was influenced by the work of Michelangelo, and the limply dangling arm of Christ in this scene may have been inspired by him. The subject's beautiful features, golden hair and exquisite jewellery in *Lady with a Unicorn* are characteristic of Raphael's portraits. This work was probably painted around 1506, but was only attributed to Raphael in 1927.

[I] **Room X:** Correggio's *Danaë* depicts an unashamedly erotic scene of the young Danaë, naked on her bed beside Cupid, receiving the god Jupiter as a shower of golden rain (the result of the encounter was their son Perseus). It is the only painting by Correggio to be found in Rome.

[J] **Room XIV:** Bernini's earliest work, from around 1615, is inconspicuously displayed on a table against a wall and shows the goat Amalthea with her foster son Zeus as a child, and a small faun. Once thought to have been a Hellenistic original, it may have been deliberately made as a forgery by Bernini. He later carved the two marble busts of Cardinal Scipione Borghese, around 1632. Also on display are three Bernini paintings, two self-portraits—one from around 1623, the other some ten years later—and his *Portrait of a Boy*.

[K] **Room XVIII:** *The Deposition*, by Rubens, was painted during his eight-year stay in Italy around 1602.

[L] **Room XX:** On view here is an early Titian masterpiece from 1514 commissioned for a wedding and showing the bride fully clothed with a nude figure of Venus. Its title, *Sacred and Profane Love*, comes from an 18th century interpretation of the two female figures rather than the artist's original intention for the painting as a whole; a celebration of both secular and spiritual love. In 1899 a private offer was made for the painting which was worth more than the estimated value of the Borghese home itself and all of its works of art. Needless to say, the offer was rejected and the painting remains on display. Three other Titian works are also exhibited, all probably painted in the 1560s: *Venus Blinding Cupid*, *St Dominic* and the *Scourging of Christ*.

in the area

Ara Pacis (*open 9-7, closed Mon, entry fee*). Located by the Tiber near Piazza Augusto Imperatore is the futuristic and contentious Ara Pacis museum, which was completed after a decade of delays in 2006 and is the first modern architectural work in Rome's *centro storico* since the 1930s. The new museum houses Ara Pacis—the superlative achievement of Augustan art—in a purpose-built unit designed by the American architect Richard Meier (b. 1934). The building is very spacious, and its glass walls and ceiling mean the monument receives a huge amount of natural light. The Ara Pacis itself is a white marble altar consecrated in 13 BC to celebrate the peace that Augustus had brought to the Empire in Spain and Gaul, and was reconstructed from original and reproduced pieces in 1937–38 on the orders of Benito Mussolini, who saw himself as a mod-

Ancient and modern meet at Ara Pacis

ern-day Caesar Augustus. The monument is carved with figures offering sacrifices to the gods. The altar's lower section is covered with intricate acanthus leaves and swans with outstretched wings. The left panel, which is almost entirely lost, represented the Lupercalia festival, while the right panel depicts Aeneas sacrificing a white sow. The left panels of the south entrance show the earth goddess Tellus as an allegory of peace, while those on the right portray a figure of the goddess Roma. The side panels illustrate the inauguration of the altar itself, with a procession that includes Augustus, his family, state officials and priests. **Map p. 75, D1**

Augustus Mausoleum. In the middle of Piazza Augusto Imperatore are the remains of the tomb of Emperor Augustus. A powerful leader, his mausoleum was one of the most sacred sites of ancient Rome. Over time, the area has been used as a fortress, amphitheatre and concert hall, before being cleared and excavations carried out in the 1930s. **Map p. 75, D1**

Galleria Nazionale D'Arte Moderna (*open 8.30–7.30, closed Mon, entry fee, Tel: 06 322 981*) Housed in a purpose-built palazzo, the gallery possesses the most important collection of Italian art dating from 1780–1960. The greatest Neoclassical sculptor, Antonio Canova, dominates the early works with his colossal statue of *Hercules and Lichas* (1815). The Impressionist Movement is represented by Van Gogh's *The Gardener* (1889) and Paul Cézanne's appealing *Le Cabanon de Jourdan* (1906). Other masterpieces include *Bronze Age* (1876) by Auguste Rodin, and one of the most important works by the Viennese Secessionist Gustav Klimt, *Three Ages of Woman* (1905). Influential 20th-century art movements are illustrated by the Dadaist artist Duchamp with his *Fountain* (1917); the Futurist artist Carlo Carrà; and the Metaphysical painter Giorgio de Chirico. Later 20th-century art is represented by Jackson Pollock, Alberto Giacometti, Cy Twombly and Afro. **Map p. 75, A2**

National Etruscan Museum (Villa Giulia) (*open 8.30–7, closed Mon, entry fee, Tel: 06 322 6571*). The beautifully-designed Villa Giulia houses an important collection devoted to pre-Roman Etruscan art. Highlights include finds from the necropolis of Vulci (Rooms 1–5), one of the most important Etruscan cities during the 7th–4th centuries BC; the delicate Sarcofago degli Sposi (Room 9), with two figures on the lid representing a husband and wife at a feast, from the 6th century BC; and the Chigi Vase (Room 17) from the early 7th century BC, depicting a lion hunt, a hare hunt and the *Judgement of Paris*, when Paris has to choose between Juno, Minerva and Venus and award the golden apple 'to the fairest'. **Map p. 75, A2**

eat

For price categories, see p. 9.

RESTAURANTS

1 €€€ Dal Bolognese, *Piazza del Popolo 1/2, Tel: 06 361 1426.* ■ In a lovely position on the expansive Piazza del Popolo and on the edge of the old artists' quarter, Dal Bolognese is the restaurant of choice for today's celebrities and high-fliers. Don't be surprised if you eat your *fritto alla Bolognese* in the company of this year's top model or hot shot lawyer but don't expect to be seated at a table outside—those are booked weeks in advance. Surprisingly unintimidating, the staff are polite and helpful and the chefs know how to prepare traditional dishes well. **Map p. 75, C1**

2 €€€ Mirabelle de l'Hotel Splendide Royal, *Via Porta Pinciana 14, Tel: 06 4216 8838.* If all restaurants could purchase their view it would be the one from the 7th floor Mirabelle. Backed by the gardens of the Villa Borghese, and looking directly out over the historic centre of Rome, the Mirabelle is certainly in an enviable position. Happily, the cuisine and service here match the view. The chef, Giuseppe Sestito, has been overseeing Mirabelle's

kitchen since 2001 and produces first class international cuisine as well as traditional Italian dishes, and the wine list has an excellent selection of mostly Italian wines. **Map p. 75, D3**

3 €€€ Il Palazzetto (*at the Hassler Hotel; see p. 11*).

4 €€€ Papà Baccus, *Via Toscana 36, Tel: 06 4274 2808.* Despite the tacky name, Papà Baccus is in fact one of the most exciting restaurants to open in Rome in recent years. Heavily influenced by Tuscan cuisine, ingredients from the region are bought in season to produce real treats such as *carabaccia* (red onion soup) and *tortelloni di patate*. Their house speciality is the Cinta Senese mixed grill, using meat from their own herd of pigs specially reared for the restaurant. **Map p. 75, C3**

5 €€ Il Margutta, *Via Margutta 118, Tel: 06 3265 0577.* A chic vegetarian restaurant which started up in the late 1970s through a passion to provide good food while promoting animal rights. It's still a thoroughly modern restaurant with bright orange walls and black sofas. The restaurant is situated on a bright corner of Via Margutta, a pleasant, quiet street in what is known as the artists' district. The Green Brunch Buffet is very good value and a good way to try out many of the vegan and vegetarian dishes available (*Mon-Sat lunchtime*), or the à la carte menu offers variations on traditional Mediterranean dishes such as rucola and champignon carpaccio or sheep's cheese in an almond crust with chicory. There is outside seating at the back of the restaurant. **Map p. 75, C2**

6 € Gina, *Via San Sebastianello 7a, Tel: 06 678 0251.* Handily located on a narrow street leading from Piazza di Spagna, Gina is the best place to pick up a *panini* to eat on the Spanish Steps or a more elaborate picnic lunch box to take to the nearby Villa Borghese. With its bright white interior, this isn't the sort of restaurant where you linger over multiple courses, more a trendy stop-off between sights. **Map p. 75, D2**

CAFÉS

7 Antico Caffè Greco, *Via Condotti 86.* ■ The coffee house of coffee houses, on the most exclusive shopping street in Rome, at the foot of the Spanish Steps. Antico Caffè Greco has been serving coffee since the 1760s. Goethe, Keats and de Chirico have all drunk here, and with reason: the red velvet furnishings, the series of small salons, the marble-top tables and the personal mementoes of past customers all add up to a unique atmosphere. If it's too busy to find a table (and it often is), a stand-up espresso at the bar is a cheaper way to take in the ambience. **Map p. 75, D2**

8 Babington's English Tea Room, *Piazza di Spagna 23.* A bastion of the very English tradition of afternoon tea, Babington's was established in 1893 (and prospered quickly during the era of the european Grand Tour) and is still managed by descendants of the same family. This charming tea room offers over 30 different types of tea to sip alongside muffins, scones and cakes. If you find yourself at Babington's outside of the teatime hour, there is also a selection of light lunches and english breakfasts to choose from. The 'rooms' still retain a 19th-century atmosphere, with dark wood furniture and prints of that period, while the open fire is welcome in the winter. The shop is well-stocked with English goodies such as jams, chutneys, fudge and chocolates. **Map p. 75, D2**

9 Caffè del Arti (*at the Galleria Nazionale d'Arte Moderna*), *Via Gramschi 73.*If you forgot to pick up your picnic lunch box from Gina's

Ornate decorations inside the coffee house of coffee houses: Antico Caffé Greco

(*see above*) then the Caffè del Arti is a good Plan B after hours enjoying the modern art on show at the neighbouring Galleria Nazionale d'Arte Moderna. Here, you can refuel on the perfectly reasonable salads and pasta on offer. However, it's the lovely terrace attached to the café which is the real draw. **Map p. 75, A2**

10 Caffè Fontana, *Via Flaminia 101-103*. A café with friendly and efficient service, necessary to keep up with the constant stream of office workers stopping by for a quick espresso at the counter, perhaps from the Ministry of Defence across the road. The room is bright, although a little worn around the edges, with five or six large tables which seem to invite conversation. Good coffee, tea, pastries and sandwiches are all available. The No. 2 tram passes outside, to and from Piazza del Popolo, and the Etruscan Museum in the Borghese gardens is close by. **Map p. 75, A1**

shop

Home to Italy's leading fashion houses, Via Condotti (**map p. 75, D2**) and Via Borgognona (**map p. 75, D2**) were once considered the most elegant streets in Rome and a home for many important craftworkers. Today, they harbour a wealth of posh shops in a proximity rarely seen outside the first twenty pages of *Vogue*. Rome vied with Paris for the title of fashion capital in the second half of the 20th century, and a stroll down these streets shows the city remains the place to make a large dent in your bank account, or at least to enjoy some superior window-shopping. The stories of the companies behind the grand designs also reveal close and interesting associations with 20th-century art and artists. For a different scene, Via Margutta (**map p. 75, C2–D2**), close to Piazza del Popolo, is the heart of the old artists' district and is the place to go for original artworks.

VIA CONDOTTI

Gucci (at no. 8) has had a boutique here since 1938. The company is on a high at present, and its new colourful and energetic designs remain as sassy and sexy as the average Roman. Years of company infighting followed founder Guccio Gucci's death in 1953, but nowadays the firm's creative director, Frida Giannini—a relative new kid on the block, and Roman to the core—is steering the firm towards more cheerful and flowery designs, away from her predecessor Texan Tom Ford's vampish and more overtly sexy collections. If you have the means, it is here that you can get your hands on some 'Genius Jeans', officially the most expensive jeans in the world, costing upwards of €3,000 for a customised pair.

At no. 10 is **Bulgari** (usually written Bvlgari, in tribute to its Greek founder, Sotirio Bulgari), a great store for watches, handbags and accessories. Bulgari jewellery design is unique, highly regarded and often imitated (and counterfeited). The firm was founded in Rome in 1884 and their flagship store was opened here in 1905, and initially sold only jewellery. The store quickly drew the world's great and good with its unique, high quality product designs which fused Greek and Roman artistic influences. Just across the Condotti at no. 92–93 is **Prada**, whose original Prada line is

Upmarket shopping on Via Condotti

now supplemented with the more earthy, relaxed and affordable Miu Miu (Miuccia Prada's nickname) range, aimed at a slightly younger audience.

Cross the Via de' Fiori to **La Perla** for the world's most luxurious underwear. At no. 76 is **Armani**, where Italy's most successful designer Giorgio continues with his timeless tailored lines. **Valentino**, over the Via Condotti at no. 13, has graceful and flattering designs from Valentino Clemente Ludovico Garavani, a man who did much to raise Rome's fashion profile to parisian heights, after opening his first atelier on this street in 1959. Valentino was a friend of

Andy Warhol, and is renowned for his extensive art collection, which includes works by Picasso, Damien Hirst and Cy Twombly.

Just off the Via Condotti, at 23 Via Bocca di Leone is **Versace**, with its brash vibrant designs. **Fendi** (at no. 39) is a Roman firm which has been operating in the city since 1925, when a young married couple, Edoardo and Adele Fendi set up a leather and fur shop on Via del Plebiscito. Their five daughters gradually took over the running of company and the shop moved to the more salubrious area of Via Condotti in the 1960s. Further up, on the corner of Via Bessiana, at no. 36, is **Fornarina**, which sells modern and funky space-age designs that recall some of David Bowie's most memorable outfits of the 1970s.

VIA BORGOGNONA

Approaching this street from the Piazza di Spagna, one first encounters **Ermenegildo Zegna** on the corner of Via Borgognona and Via de' Fiori (no. 7), which sells beautifully tailored high-end suits. There is another Gucci store on the corner facing it, followed by the world´s most exclusive (and counterfeited) bag and suitcase designer **Louis Vuitton** (no. 6–6a). The next store along from here is **Fratelli Rossetti** at no. 5, which sells a selection of fashionable leather footwear and accessories for men and women (their men's loafers have been described as 'indestructible').

On the other side of the Via Borgognona is **Roberto Cavalli** (no. 25). Cavalli has an interesting background for the art fan, as his grandfather was a significant painter of the Macchiaioli School, forerunners of the Impressionists from 1860 (see p. 149). His grandson's designs are brasher, however, and recall Versace, with extensive use of animal print, as well as leather and denim patches. His upfront, sexy clothes are also available at more reasonable rates, through his Just Cavalli and Roberto Cavalli Class ranges.

Loro Piana, at no. 31, is celebrated for its high quality cashmeres and other luxury goods. Finally, on the corner of Via Borgognona and Via Bocca di Leone is **Moschino**, whose eclectic, off the wall and sometimes punky designs have led the company´s mastermind, the late Francisco Moschino, to become known as the closest thing to an Italian Jean Paul Gaultier. Moschino garments often add whimsical and witty elements to classical designs, and the Cheap & Chic brand offers more affordable alternatives.

VIA MARGUTTA & VIA DEL BABUINO

Via Margutta, the old artists' district of Rome, is a pretty back street behind Via del Babuino. In 1634 a census revealed that out of the 244 artists working in Rome that year, 104 lived in this area; most of them French, Dutch and Flemish painters taking advantage of the then tax-free status of the quarter. Nowadays, the street is peaceful and creeper-clad and has a selection of attractive courtyards and gardens to peer into, as well as plenty of modern furniture and antique shops to browse. At no. 53 is a complex of artists studios (mostly reconstructed in the 19th century) with a garden. The Italian film director Federico Fellini lived at no. 110 until his death in 1993. Street fairs in spring and autumn exhibit local and international artists.

The sprawling **TAD concept store**, at Via del Babuino no. 155/a (**map p. 75, D2**), is a world away from the Via Condotti's single-brand designer stores and may well be Rome's most exciting place to shop. This 1000m square haven of contemporary cool is housed on two levels, employs informed and friendly assistants and takes fash-ion, interior design and presenta-tion very seriously indeed. Although TAD bills itself as an 'ethnic' insti-tution, and sells gems and crystals, no flaky bohemian clichés apply here. Quite the contrary, TAD is innovative yet light-hearted, and has stocked such brands as the übercool Balenciaga, Brit designer Hussein Chalayan, and Italians Angelo Figus and Alberto Biani. The store also designs and produces its own collections, and holds music events, along with regular exhibi-tions of contemporary art, some of which is available to buy. As for the tastebuds, there is also a café.

PIAZZA NAVONA

introduction

This lively district of narrow cobbled streets and graceful Renaissance palaces includes the sublime Pantheon, churches with Caravaggio masterpieces, shopping opportunities in and around the Campo dei Fiori and many great restaurants near the focal Piazza Navona, where Bernini's extravagant Fountain of the Four Rivers steals the show.

Just off the square are the San Luigi dei Francesi and the Sant'Agostino churches, both of which contain fabulous early works by Caravaggio.

The ancient and incomparable Pantheon, possibly Rome's most stunning building, lies just to the east of Piazza Navona, while Campo dei Fiori to the south has a fantastic morning market, and a vibrant atmosphere by night. The nearby Palazzo Farnese is Rome's finest renaissance palace, built for the man who later excommunicated England's Henry VIII.

Santa Maria sopra Minerva is the city's only Gothic church and is home to Michelangelo's transcendent sculpture of the *Risen Christ*, and the Palazzo Altemps houses an impressive state-owned collection of treasures from antiquity.

Meanwhile, the Ghetto area is the perfect place for a stroll and to sample some Jewish-influenced Roman cuisine.

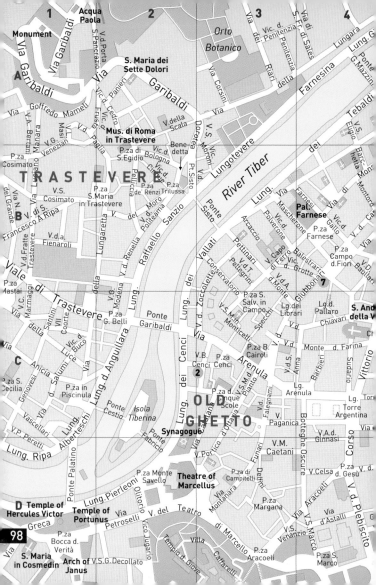

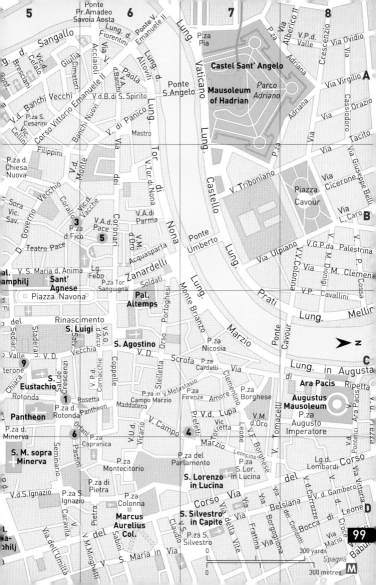

Piazza Navona

Map: p.99, C5 **Highlights:** Fountain of the Four Rivers by Bernini; façade of Sant'Agnese in Agone by Borromini

The long, narrow Piazza Navona follows the dimensions of the ancient Stadium of Domitian, where athletic games—the Agones Capitolini—were held from AD 86 in front of 30,000 spectators. The square's original name *In Agone* comes from the Greek word for sports contests, *agones*. These days, the square plays host to street artists and buskers who entertain locals and visitors alike at restaurant tables. In the centre are three magnificent fountains, and the piazza is framed by stately palaces and churches. Side streets lead off towards wonderfully authentic Roman restaurants (*see p. 110*).

Al fresco dining on Piazza Navona

a/s/e Rome

The central **Fountain of the Four Rivers** (*Fontana dei Quattro Fiumi*) is one of Bernini's most famous works. Bernini was initially excluded from entering a design for the fountain but in 1648 Pope Innocent X was unable to resist commissioning his phenomenal plan to decorate Piazza Navona with a fountain to support the obelisk that had been lying in pieces for centuries at the Circus of Maxentius on the Appian Way. Its four colossal allegorical figures, carved by Bernini's assistants, represent the most renowned rivers of the four continents then known: the Danube, the Ganges, the Nile and the River Plate. The obelisk is crowned with a dove, Innocent X's family emblem.

On the west side of the piazza is the church of **Sant'Agnese in Agone** (*open 9–12 & 4–7 except Mon morning*), one of the key works of Bernini's main rival, Francesco Borromini. Although Borromini did not complete it (he fell out of favour with Innocent X's successor, Alexander VII), he did provide the wonderful concave façade. A popular tale regards Bernini and Borromini to have been such rivals that the fountain's River Plate figure holds up an arm to protect himself from the unstable belfry of Sant'Agnese. The fountain was in fact unveiled in 1651, two years before Borromini began work on the church.

San Luigi dei Francesi

Open: 7.30–12.30 & 3.30–7, closed Thur pm **Charges:** Free entry
Map: p. 99, C5
Highlight: St Matthew triptych by Caravaggio

The French national church in Rome (1518–89) houses the Contarelli Chapel (the last on the left), which contains Caravaggio's first public commission: a cycle of paintings depicting scenes from the life of **St Matthew**, which the rebellious genius painted for this chapel in 1597–1603. The three works, which made the artist a sensation in Rome, represent a seismic shift in the history of Western art, away from the affected style of Mannerism to a more naturalistic approach (*see box on p. 103*).

The *Calling of St Matthew* depicts the story of the tax collector-turned-apostle being 'shown the light' by Jesus, from the *Gospel of St Matthew 9:9*: "Jesus saw a man named Matthew at his seat in the custom house, and said to him, 'Follow me', and Matthew rose and followed him". The beam emanating from Jesus miraculously cuts through the shadowy *chiaroscuro*, and the gloomy chapel itself, showing the artist's theatrical instincts, and ushering in the Baroque era.

The *Inspiration of St Matthew* in the centre shows how an angel supposedly visited to offer guidance to the apostle and evangelist as he wrote. The *Martyrdom of St Matthew* shows the saint's death at the hands of an assassin ordered by the King of Ethiopia. The artist himself stands centre left, behind the murderer. X-rays have revealed that Caravaggio attempted two less inventive compositions on the canvas, only later returning to the subject with renewed confidence after producing the other two paintings in the chapel.

Sant'Agostino

Open: 7.45–12.00 & 4.30–7.30 **Charges:** Free entry **Map:** p. 99, C6
Highlights: *Madonna di Loreto* by Caravaggio; *Prophet Isaiah* fresco by Raphael; Tomb of St Monica

Just to the northeast of Piazza Navona is Sant'Agostino, a plainly elegant early Renaissance church from 1493, with a façade of marble from the Colosseum. The church contains one of the most beautiful, but least-known paintings by Caravaggio in Rome: the **Madonna di Loreto** (1604), which is located on the altar in the Cavalletti Chapel in the corner to the left of the entrance.

The peasants' bare feet and the humble nature of the house from which the Madonna emerges to meet the pilgrims caused a furore when the work was first unveiled to the public. The outsized baby Jesus compellingly represents the Madonna's metaphorical burden and Caravaggio's skill beautifully catches a meeting of the everyday with the divine.

Caravaggio 1571–1610

Michelangelo Merisi da Caravaggio is now credited as being one of the greatest revolutionaries in Italian art. He was, to borrow a phrase from another era, 'mad, bad and dangerous to know' and his paintings, especially in later works, are often austere and dramatic, filled with emphatic action and psychological intensity, qualities that he himself embodied.

Caravaggio was born and trained in the northern province of Lombardy which had an artistic tradition of realism. At the age of 20, he moved to Rome. Here, he became interested in portraying scenes from everyday life: the tricksters, players and gypsies of the poor quarters that he frequented. It was this interest in 'real life' and people that made his work so revolutionary. He once said, 'Everything in art that is not taken from life is trifling.' He applied this modern approach to religious themes, often portraying biblical characters in a realistic, human way that people were not used to, and church authorities were not comfortable with—three of the five major altarpieces he painted for Roman churches were rejected.

He was made famous by his *St Matthew* triptych (1597–1603), painted for the church of San Luigi dei Francesi. These artworks caused a sensation when they were first shown because of their acutely observed details, dynamic action and the beautiful and moving way Caravaggio used deep shadow and directional light.

In 1606 he killed a man in a brawl over a bet, and had to flee Rome. He spent the rest of his life on the run in Naples, Malta and Sicily, but he continued to produce astounding works of art under the protection of powerful people and families. Eventually, in 1610, seeking a pardon from the pope, he set off for Rome but died on the way from malaria, contracted on the beach near Porto Ercole in western Tuscany.

As well as the churches of San Luigi dei Francesi and Sant'Agostino, his masterpieces can be seen in the Galleria Borghese, Santa Maria del Popolo, Galleria Doria Pamphilj, and the Pinacoteca Capitolina.

Raphael's *Prophet Isaiah* fresco is located on the third pillar on the left side of the nave. Painted in 1512, it is thought that Raphael was influenced by the figures Michelangelo had just finished painting on the Sistine Chapel ceiling.

In the chapel to the left of the choir is the **tomb of St Monica**, the long-suffering mother of St Augustine who was ill-treated by a drunken husband. A devout Christian, she later followed her son to Milan where he was converted and baptised. Fittingly, she is now the patron saint of patience, mothers, wives and victims of abuse.

The Pantheon

Open: Mon–Sat 8.30–7.30, Sun 9–6 **Charges:** Free entry **Tel:** 06 6830 0230 **Map:** p. 99, C5
Highlights: The dome; Raphael's tomb

No building has had a greater impact on western architecture than the breathtaking Pantheon, the best preserved of all ancient Roman buildings and the most magnificent symbol of the Empire. The present structure, in constant use since its construction on Emperor Hadrian's instructions in AD 125, was dedicated as a shrine to all the planetary gods (*pan theon*). In 609 the Pantheon became the first of Rome's temples to be Christianised.

Piazza della Rotonda, in front of the Pantheon holds numerous cafés which put tables outside for most of the year, and are almost always full. The square has acquired a relaxed and typically Roman atmosphere.

The Interior

The impact of the Pantheon's cavernous interior is staggering, and the way that sunlight shines in through the 9-metre opening in the roof is a feat of undiluted architectural brilliance. The **dome**, made of concrete, was the largest vault ever built, while the height and diame-

The Pantheon dome: the largest vault ever built

ter of the echoing interior are both 43.3m. Precious marbles decorate the floor and the ceilings. The gilded bronze which once lined the ceiling was taken and melted down to make Bernini's canopy above the main altar in St Peter's in the 17th century. The majority of the original coloured marble on the walls remains, and the floor, though restored, keeps its original design.

The third niche on the left side of the building is the **tomb of Raphael**, who was buried here at his request. Below the empty niche to the right is the short epitaph of his fiancée Maria Bibbiena, the daughter of a cardinal, who died before their wedding.

Santa Maria sopra Minerva

> **Open:** 7–7 **Charges:** Free entry **Map:** p. 99, D5
> **Highlights:** *The Risen Christ* by Michelangelo; tombs of Maria Raggi and St Catherine of Siena; frescoes by Filippino Lippi

Santa Maria sopra Minerva was built from 1280–1370 over a 1st-century BC temple to Minerva, the Roman goddess of craft and wisdom. Although the interior is thought of today as a little gaudy, with its colourful rose windows and 19th-century restored decorations, it remains of great interest as Rome's only Gothic church, and for the artistic treasures that it houses.

Michelangelo's statue of ***The Risen Christ*** (completed in 1521) is to the left of the altar, and shows Christ holding the Crucifix firmly, reflecting the certainty of his convictions. The statue is rendered with great delicacy and Michelangelo was paid what was considered a small fortune for the commission (200 ducats). Towards the rear exit is the pavement tomb of the early Renaissance painter Fra' Angelico: the humble Florentine died in the convent of the church in 1455. On the second nave pillar is the **tomb of Maria Raggi** (1642), by Bernini; the flowing drape effect and use of coloured marble were techniques which the sculptor was to develop throughout his career.

On the right side is the Carafa Chapel, with **frescoes by Filippino Lippi** of the Virgin and St Thomas Aquinas . Particularly beautiful are

Brightly coloured stained glass inside Santa Maria sopra Minerva, restored in the 19th century

the group of angels in his *Assumption* on the altar wall.

Under the high altar is the **tomb of St Catherine of Siena**. She was a great campaigner for church reform, and wrote countless letters on the subject to Pope Gregory XI eventually persuading him to return to Rome and therefore reinstate the papal office in the city. She died in the church building in 1380 and was decreed the patron saint of Italy in 1939.

Since 2001, the basilica has been the titular church in Rome of the Archbishop of Westminster (England).

In the piazza outside is a charming sculpture of an elephant by Bernini, supporting an obelisk from the *Isaeum Campense*, or Temple of Isis, which stood nearby.

in the area

Palazzo Altemps (*open 9–7.45, closed Mon, entry fee, Tel: 06 3996 7700*). Palazzo Altemps houses a beautifully displayed collection of ancient Roman sculptures, most notably the Ludovisi Throne. Highlights on the ground floor include the bronze head of Marcus Aurelius in Room 5, and the remains of the Medieval tower in Room 6. On the first floor, beautiful reliefs along the gallery lead to Room 19, bright with frescoes, that contains a striking statue of the messenger of the gods, Hermes (c. AD 100). Room 20 contains two important statue groups and a seated male. Room 21 is home to the renowned Ludovisi Throne, a block of white marble carved with bas-reliefs. Most experts place the throne as a Western Greek work c. 460 BC, due to its mix of Archaic and Early Classical styles. The central relief shows Aphrodite rising from the sea, aided by two attendants.
Map p. 99, C6

Testing the legend of the Bocca della Verità (Mouth of Truth)

Bocca della Verità (*open 10–1 and 3–5 or 2.30–6.30, donation requested*). In the porch of Santa Maria in Cosmedin is the large, marble face of Bocca della Verità, the 'Mouth of Truth'. Possibly depicting one of the pagan gods, legend relates that the open mouth will close on any liar's hand placed into it. The stone is in fact an ancient manhole cover and was put in its current place in 1632, but visitors to Rome still arrive here in their droves to test the legend and queue to have their photos taken. Santa Maria in Cosmedin itself is a fine example of a Roman medieval church and traces of 11th-century frescoes can be seen inside. Opposite the church, across the piazza (which is actually a busy road), are the ancient temples of Portunus (the god of harbours) and of Hercules Victor (a popular idol for traders), both dating from the end of the 2nd century BC, which have survived remarkably well. **Map p. 98, D1**

Palazzo Farnese (*not open to visitors*). On Piazza Navona, this is the most magnificent Renaissance palace in Rome and is now the French Embassy. It was designed by Antonio da Sangallo the Younger for Cardinal Alessandro Farnese, who later became Pope Paul III and excommunicated King Henry VIII of England in 1538. Michelangelo finished the upper storeys and added the distinctive cornice at the top. **Map p. 98, B4**

Old Ghetto. This is perhaps the most atmospheric district of central Rome. The city's Jewish community was segregated here from 1556. The walls of the Ghetto were torn down only in 1848 and the houses demolished in 1888. Mussolini introduced anti-Semitic laws in the 1930s and 2,091 Roman Jews perished in the Holocaust. The commanding Synagogue was built in 1899–1904 by Vincenzo Costa and Osvaldo Armanni, on the ruins of the former Ghetto. It houses a Jewish Museum of Art (*open Sun–Fri 10–5, closed Sat, entry fee*) containing silver and textiles from the 17th–19th centuries, as well as a marble Holy Ark dating from 1523 and incorporating some Roman fragments. **Map p. 98, C3**

Theatre of Marcellus (*open 9–6, free entry*). Just the façade remains of a theatre planned by Julius Caesar, in 13 or 11 BC dedicated by Augustus to his nephew and son-in-law, Marcellus, who died in 23 BC aged 19. Baldassare Peruzzi converted the remains of the theatre, which would have held around 15,000 spectators, into a palace for one of Rome's noble families in the 16th century. He also constructed the façade's curved exterior. The palazzo remains a fine example of a later building contained within a Roman building. Next to the theatre are three columns from the Temple of Apollo Medico, dedicated in 433 BC to the healing god Apollo. A hospital dedicated to Apollo's son Aesculapius stood on the nearby island in the Tiber, where one still stands today. **Map p. 98, D2**

eat

This is *the* eating district of Rome with the largest selection and concentration of restaurants and cafés in the city. Piazza Navona (**map p. 99, C5**) and its surrounding streets are the hub of gastronomic activity, especially at night when the square comes into its own with craft stalls packing the centre while restaurants line the outside. Here, it seems, any dining experience can be found from top class restaurants with prices to match, to cosy *trattorie* where Roman specialities are cooked from handed-down recipes. To the south of Piazza Navona is the Old Ghetto, on the river, an area which offers some excellent opportunities to eat Jewish-inspired Roman dishes. During the day, Campo dei Fiori (*see p. 115*) has one of the best fruit and vegetable markets in the city. It closes at 1pm, but usually begins to wind down after midday when the square's cafés begin to fill up. For price categories, see p. 9.

RESTAURANTS

1 €€€ La Rosetta, *Via della Rosetta 8*, Tel: 06 68 61 002. This has long been considered the premiere place to eat fish in Rome. The Michelin starred restaurant is in an attractive building and has the benefit of being centrally located: just metres from Piazza della Rotonda and the Pantheon. The dishes are exquisitely prepared, using the freshest of ingredients: the *baccalà e carciofini con menta* (salt cod with artichokes and mint) and *scampi scottati con zucchine allo zenzero* (grilled langoustine with zucchini and ginger) cannot be missed. An equally excellent list of wines and champagne accompanies the menu. **Map p. 99, C6**

2 €€ Piperno, *Monte dei Cenci 9*, Tel: 06 68 80 6629. ■ A bastion of Jewish cuisine, Piperno has been serving food in the same premises in the Old Ghetto region of the city since the 1860s. The interior is evocative of that time with its panelled dado and 19th century paintings on the walls. The house speciality is *carciofi alla giudia* (Jewish-style artichokes, deep-fried in a light batter) and is deservedly popular. However, for the more stout of heart they also prepare an excellent selection of offal: sweetbreads, oxtail and tripe are all on offer. The waiting staff are helpful and hardworking. Reservations recommended. Closed August. **Map p. 98, C3**

3 **€ Da Francesco**, *Piazza del Fico 29. Tel: 06 686 4009*. Walking into Da Francesco is like walking into a friend's house that is full of guests. There is bustle and chatter and you sit where there is space, often squeezing onto the end of a large table of Italian diners, and drinks are served almost immediately. Menus appear on the table but are not often used. Tomato and mozzarella or prosciutto are good *antipasti*, and the house speciality is excellent thin and crispy pizza *alla romana* with sparing toppings of mushroom, cheese or ham. There is a good buffet for vegetables. If there isn't space inside, there are tables and chairs outside with heaters when the weather is colder. **Map p. 99, B5**

4 **€ Gino**, *Vicolo Rossini, Tel: 06 68 73 434*. Hidden behind ivy on this narrow lane and distinguishable only by its specials board outside the door, Gino's is a popular place worth seeking out as it is one of only a few old-style neighbourhood *trattorie* left in the *centro storico*. The interior is snug and inviting and the food traditional with Roman dishes such as pasta *a cacio e pepe* (a simple dish with grated Pecorino cheese and lots of black pepper) or *frito misto alla romana* (fried meat and vegetables). It is worth arriving early or booking a table in advance. Closed Sundays. **Map p. 99, C7**

Dried herb mixes on sale in Campo dei Fiori

Relaxing on Campo dei Fiori after the busy market has closed for the day

Herbs

Imagine you are soon to leave the city where 75 per cent of the restaurants are good and the rest are fantastic and, naturally enough, you want to ensure that you can create a few authentic Italian dishes on your return home, without exceeding your baggage allowance. *Erbe* (herbs) are the answer, and a vast array of them are available at Rome's markets, larger gourmet shops and *erboriste* (herb specialists). Often they are sold in dried form, very handy for packing in your suitcase.

Basilico (basil) is an aromatic herb fundamental to Italian soups and tomato or pesto sauces. The flat-leaf variety of parsley, *prezzemolo*, is typically used, and is good with almost any dish, and also as a breath freshener after garlic. *Origano* (oregano) can season pizzas and vegetable dishes while the aromatic *rosmarino* (rosemary) works well with *salvio* (sage) as a seasoning for roasts, potatoes, breads and vegetable dishes. *Salvio* is also used to season veal, liver and pork, or its leaves can be dipped in a light batter, fried and served with wine as an antipasto. *Finocchio* (fennel) comes in flat *femmina* (female) and rounder *maschio* (male) forms. The latter is better suited to cookery, while the *maschio* can be eaten raw, with or without olive oil and fresh lemon juice. *Lauro* (bay leaf) is a good all-rounder, and its woody flavour goes particularly well with stews, sauces, and grilled meats, as does that of *timo* (thyme), which works with marinades and seafood too.

You will also see a myriad of herb mixes geared to making specific sauces: *Puttanesca* comes from the Italian 'puttana' meaning prostitute, as, with pasta, it was a quick meal to be eaten between clients; it contains garlic, capers, black olives, anchovies and tomatoes, and is a slightly spicy—and typically Roman—sauce. *Amatriciana*, a tomato and bacon sauce from Amatrice, to the northeast of Rome, is traditionally served with *bucatini* (hollow spaghetti). *Arrabiata* is a very spicy tomato sauce with a good measure of *peperoncini rossi* (strong red peppers). If you still have any doubts, just ask one of Rome's effusive stallholders.

CAFES

5 **Antico Caffè della Pace**, *Via della Pace 3/7*. This cafe commands a supreme corner vantage point in this winding, intimate part of Navona, and you will be fortunate if you can claim a highly prized seat outside. However, the inside is just as pleasing; cool in summer and cosy in winter with it's beautiful dark wood interior, marble top tables and elegant mirrors. The bar staff are attractive, willowy types who provide efficient and friendly service. This is one of the best places in the area to have a drink and spend a moment to sit back and enjoy being in Rome. **Map p. 99, B6**

6 **La Casa del Caffè**, *Via degli Orfani 84*. The retro sign stretching across the front of the building is a piece of work in itself, while the café inside is a friendly place and not too busy considering the crowds around the corner at the Pantheon. Fresh coffee is ground at the back in huge vats and gives the café an inviting atmosphere. Coffee served here is no-frills in well-used glasses but is good. **Map p. 99, C5**

7 **The Grill and Caffé**, *Via Giubbonari 54*. After the market on Campo dei Fiore closes at 1pm and the *trattorie* around the square

begin to fill up, this is a great place to relax and look out over the square with a chocolate croissant and a cappuccino. The café is set back slightly from the main square which means that you can experience the hustle and bustle from a slightly better vantage point than the cafés on the piazza itself. In the evening it serves (expensive) cocktails. **Map p. 98, B4**

8 **Pascucci**, *Via di Torre Argentina 20*. On a busy street near the Pantheon, Pascucci is famous for its delicious fruit shakes which it has been making since the 1930s. The fruity concoctions make a refreshing change from ice-cream. It's also a lively place to have a typical Roman breakfast of coffee and pastries. **Map p. 98, C4**

9 **Sant'Eustachio-il caffè**, *Piazza Sant'Eustachio 82*. There is nothing quite like turning the corner into a quiet piazza and coming across a happy, animated crowd of people standing outside a tiny café to make you want to join in. Sant'Eustachio is such a place. The concept is simple—black, sweet coffee (if you don't want sugar you need to ask for a *caffè amaro*), lively conversation and a pretty setting. **Map p. 99, C5**

A typical cul de sac near Campo dei Fiori

shop

The bustling market square of **Campo dei Fiori (map p. 98, B4)** is home to one of the oldest fruit, vegetable and flower markets in the city, which has opened its stalls here every morning since 1869. As well as being a treasure trove for herbs and spices (*see box on p. 113*), the market also sells essential Roman kitchen items such as garlic presses and balsamic vinegar dispensers, alongside souvenir bags, aprons and tacky tourist T-shirts.

Although the 'Field of Flowers' was christened in medieval times, after the abandoned square had become a flowery meadow, Campo dei Fiori has been a centre for trade and commerce since the 15th century, a legacy illustrated in the names of the streets leading off from the piazza, which refer to various trades: Via dei Giubbonari, (tailors); Via dei Cappellari, (hat-makers); and Via dei Chiavari (key-makers).

By the 16th century, the area had become a prestigious residential district and red, blue and orange palazzi still frame the square. The almost

a/s/e

incongruous statue of Giordano Bruno, who was burned alive here in 1600 for espousing scientific views, solemnly peers down over proceedings, and whispers of the square's darker past as a site for public executions. Perhaps this goes some way to explain the fact that this is the only piazza in Rome without a church. The square's name is suitably honoured with lovely flower stalls by the fountain at the north end.

Taba, on the west side of the piazza, has been selling ethnic ponchos, hats, candles and bags to a world music soundtrack for over a decade. Its perpetually rolling stock mainly comes from Thailand and South America, and although not notably Roman, the pashminas are said to be the cheapest in the city. On the other side of the square is **Antica Norcineria Viola**, at no. 43, a family institution which has been here since 1880, with a huge selection of cured hams, wild boar sausages, prosciutto and pancetta from Lazio and beyond. With many local specialities, the shop satisfies the gastronomic demands of local gourmands and tourists alike, and best of all, they are likely to offer you a taste before you buy, then expertly wrap up your choice in lilac paper. The **Delicatessen** snugly located in the square's south corner, at no. 17, bills itself rather modestly as selling 'typical italian products'. Fortunately, this means many varieties and flavours of balsamic vinegar, fine chocolates, coffee and crusty bread. The extensive wine selection gives options for every budget, although the 'Il Duce' may be one to miss if Mussolini's taste in wine was anything like his taste in architecture.

True to name, Via dei Giubbonari contains numerous clothes shops. On the right, twenty metres from the square is **Habana**, at no. 45, which combines elegant local tailoring and affordable prices with charming service. Next door, at no. 44, **Funaro Alessandra**, has similarly choice goods, with a slightly more surly edge. On the left-hand side of the road are two very trendy **children's shoe shops** at nos. 51 and 63.

Just to the north of Campo dei Fiori leads Via del Pellegrino. **Sciam**, at no. 55, is a treasure trove of coloured glassware. The owner, Youssef, started the shop 30 years ago, importing glass from Syria and Egypt, and fills the premises to bursting. Baskets of beads line the floor, light-shades hang from the ceiling and walls, and wooden crates of vases, glasses and ornaments are stacked down the narrow stairs and into three rooms in the cellar. It's difficult to resist sifting through the turquoise, orange, emerald and ruby hoard.

A hard day's shopping at Campo dei Fiori

THE VATICAN

introduction

Located on the west of the Tiber, the Vatican City is understandably one of the most visited places in Rome, and the artistic treasures here are a draw for art aficionados and pilgrims alike. St Peter's Basilica is a High Renaissance masterpiece, thanks to contributions to its outstanding beauty from many of Rome's leading lights, including Bernini, Michelangelo and Carlo Maderno. The grottoes underneath the basilica, meanwhile, reveal the fascinating origins of this great monument of western Christendom

The Vatican museums contain a vast array of artistic riches with which only the Louvre in Paris or the Hermitage in St Petersburg could hope to compete, and the Sistine Chapel, with its sublime ceiling by Michelangelo, still stands as the supreme symbol of individual artistic achievement.

The Vatican City itself is the world's smallest independent state, occupying less than half a square kilometre, but operates as the nerve centre of the world's largest religious organisation. Castel Sant'Angelo began as a Mausoleum for Emperor Hadrian and has a fascinating history, including its use as a fortress in the Middle Ages and its decoration by Bernini in the 17th century. The charming Borgo Pio near the area's principal sights is a sedate street to stop for an ice cream or some lunch in between gorging on all the art.

ST PETER'S SQUARE

St Peter's Square (*map p. 120, C3*) is a work of undiluted brilliance by Gian Lorenzo Bernini and a fine example of Roman civic architecture, providing a fitting approach to the world's largest and most revered church. The view down the broad Via della Conciliazione—completed during Mussolini's reign—is equally captivating, while the horsedrawn carriages that queue here add to the square's charm. The street is named after the pact of 1929 when the Vatican was recognised as an independent state and renounced all hope of regaining the temporal power it had previously enjoyed since the Middle Ages. In the centre of the piazza, on a tall plinth, is a 25.5m obelisk brought from Alexandria in AD 37. It is the only obelisk in Rome that has no hieroglyphics. The two elegant fountains in the square were designed by Carlo Maderno in 1614 (on the right), and Bernini in 1667 (on the left).

A bird's eye view of St Peter's Square, designed by Bernini

St Peter's Basilica

Open: Basilica 7–7, Oct–March 7–6; dome 8–5.45, Oct–March
8–4.45, often closed on Wed am when the Pope is in the basilica
Charges: Free entry **Map:** p. 120, C2
Highlights: Bronze door from old St Peter's; Cathedra of St Peter
by Bernini; *Pietà* by Michelangelo
Services: Mass is held on Sun at 8.30, 9, 10, 11, 12 & 5. Holy
Communion can be received in the Cappella del Santissimo
Sacramento throughout the day on Sun.
*NB: Shorts, mini-skirts and bare shoulders are forbidden inside St
Peter's and the Vatican City.*

St Peter's is both an architectural masterpiece and Rome's most popular spiritual site. It occupies the site of a basilica begun by Emperor
Constantine on the spot where St Peter was buried after his martyrdom. In the mid-15th century the papacy decided to rebuild the
church on an even grander scale, and leading architects were still
contributing to this enterprise into the early 17th century.

Through the black gate at the left end of the portico is an equestrian statue of Charlemagne, the first Holy Roman Emperor. On the
right is a statue of Constantine I, by Bernini. Constantine made
Christianity the official state religion in AD 324.

The basilica's perfect proportions disguise the enormity of its 186m
by 137m interior. The gilded coffered ceiling was designed by
Bramante, the architect who pulled down most of the old basilica and
began a complete reconstruction, earning for himself the nickname
'Bramante ruinante'. The magnificent central **bronze door**, completed
in 1445, is from the old St Peter's, and is decorated with reliefs
depicting Jesus, the Virgin Mary, St Peter and St Paul by the
Florentine artist, sculptor and architect Filarete.

Highlights of the interior of the basilica are given below and
marked on the plan on p. 123.

St Peter's

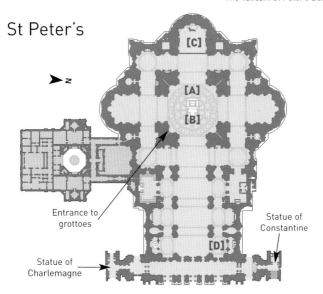

Entrance to grottoes

Statue of Constantine

Statue of Charlemagne

[A] The dome
[B] The high altar

[C] Cathedra of St Peter
[D] Michelangelo's *Pietà*

[A] **The dome:** Michelangelo's dome is an architectural masterpiece. Uncomplicated, imposing, and filled with light, it ascends directly above the tomb in which St Peter's remains were found. It was completed after Michelangelo's death. It is possible to climb the dome; a lift and staircase go up to the roof from an entrance outside the basilica.

[B] **High altar:** Over the high altar, which in turn stands directly above the tomb of St Peter, rises the great canopy, designed by Bernini and unveiled by Urban VIII in 1633. This enormous Baroque structure, a blend of architecture and decorative sculpture, was cast in bronze taken from the Pantheon and is said to be the world's largest bronze piece. Four gilt-bronze columns rise from marble plinths, which are decorated with the Barberini bees—the family emblem of Urban VIII. At the top of the canopy is the Holy Spirit, represented as a dove in a circle of light. A chorus of angels surround the dove.

[C] **Cathedra of St Peter:** At the back of the church, two steps from the old basilica lead to the raised tribune, with the Cathedra of St Peter (1665). This huge gilt-bronze throne, enclosing an ancient wooden chair said to have belonged to St Peter is a typically flamboyant composition by Bernini. The throne is supported by statues of St Augustine and St Ambrose (of the Latin church), as well as St Athanasius and St John Chrysostom (representing the Greek church).

[D] **Michelangelo's *Pietà*:** The most famous sculpture in the church is Michelangelo's beautiful *Pietà*, in the first chapel in the right aisle. The previously unknown Michelangelo made this work in 1499 at the age of

Michelangelo's famous *Pietà* in St Peter's basilica

24. It is perhaps the most touching of all his sculptures, and the only one inscribed with his name, on the ribbon on Mary's left shoulder. A Dante verse probably inspired him to represent the Madonna as younger than Jesus: '*Virgin mother, daughter of your son...*'. The composition works so well that we don't notice how small Christ is in relation to his mother: Mary's left hand echoes the movement of Christ's left leg; Mary's head leans forward as Christ's tilts back; and the curve of her dress is repeated by his limp right arm.

Vatican Grottoes

Open: 7–6, Oct–March 7–5. Group tours of the necropolis and the tomb of St Peter most days 9–12 and 2–5. Apply at Ufficio Scavi, left of St Peter's, Mon–Fri 9–5 **Charges:** Free entry **Tel:** 06 6988 5318 **Map:** p. 120, C2
Highlight: Tomb of St Peter

Beneath St Peter's are the so-called Vatican Grottoes. They are only partially open to the public, but the tombs of many popes can be seen here, including that of the only Englishman ever to hold papal office: Nicholas Breakspear, who reigned as Hadrian IV (1154–59). The finest of the tombs, artistically speaking, is probably that of Pius VI (d. 1799), a magnificent kneeling statue by Canova. The simple tomb slab of John Paul II, who was buried here on 8th April 2005, is now a permanent pilgrimage site.

   A mosaic at the heart of the grottoes marks the **tomb of St Peter**, which lies beneath. The remains of a necropolis here, dating from the 1st century, were discovered in 1940. A wall, scratched by pilgrims praying for aid from St Peter, was also found, and behind it, in 1965, were discovered the bones of an elderly, thickset man. They were at once declared to be those of St Peter, making this one of the most sacred shrines of Christianity.

Vatican Museums

Open: March–Oct Mon–Fri 10–3.30 (last exit 4.45), Sat 10–1.30 (last exit 2.45), Nov–Feb Mon–Sat 10–12.30 (last exit 1.45), closed Sun except last of month 9–12.30 (last exit at 1.45), closed on certain Holy days **Charges:** Entry fee except for last Sun of month **Tel:** 06 6988 3333 (recorded message in English/Italian) or 06 6988 4947 (English spoken) **Map:** p. 120, B2
Highlights: Raphael Rooms; Sistine Chapel; Ancient Greek and Roman sculpture in the Chiaramonti Museum

The Vatican Museums contain the famous Sistine Chapel, frescoed by Michelangelo, and the Raphael Rooms, entirely designed by Raphael. The museums also contain some of the world's greatest art treasures, and are without equal in terms of range and quality. An unrivalled collection of ancient Greek and Roman sculpture, an important picture gallery, and early Christian art are all displayed in magnificently decorated halls and chapels (*see plan on pp. 128–129*).

The 'Sistine Route'

In order to control the flow of visitors to the Sistine Chapel, the Vatican authorities have imposed a fixed route around many of the museums. It is a tiring and long route but is the only way to see the Sistine Chapel and Raphael Rooms. From the Quattro Cancelli two flights of stairs lead up to Bramante's long west gallery. From here you can proceed through numerous other galleries to the Raphael Rooms, and from there to the Sistine Chapel. The other Vatican museums must be visited before joining the 'Sistine Route'.

RAPHAEL ROOMS

Julius II dismissed all of his other painters in order to commission the 25-year-old Raphael to decorate this suite of papal chambers, which he used as his own residence. The Raphael Rooms (*Stanze di Raffaello*) are the painters' masterpiece and show his artistic development from 1508 to his death in 1520. Raphael began work in the

Stanza della Segnatura (II), before continuing to the Stanza d'Eliodoro (III), the Stanza dell'Incendio (I), and the Sala di Costantino (IV). The rooms today are unfortunately crowded, being on a particularly cramped section of the route.

Room IV (Sala di Costantino):
Giulio Romano, Raphael's pupil, painted this room after Raphael's death, working to designs planned by Raphael. On the wall facing the window is the *Victory of Constantine over Maxentius near the Milvian Bridge*, a defining moment in the history of the Christian Church (*see p. 17*). On the entrance wall is the *Vision of the Cross*, depicting what Constantine saw before the battle: a heavenly cross with the words '*with this sign you will conquer*'. On the wall opposite the entrance is the *Baptism of Constantine.* On the window wall is *Constantine's Donation of Rome to Pope Sylvester*, which was used as propaganda for the foreign diplomats and monarchs made to wait here, although the document allegedly making the donation was later proved a forgery. The ceiling painting shows the *Triumph of Christianity.* Just off Room IV is the **Room of the Chiaroscuri** with a beautiful carved and gilded ceiling, and the adjoining **Chapel of Nicholas V** with wonderful frescoes covering the entire room by Fra' Angelico (1448–50).

Room III (Stanza d'Eliodoro):
Raphael painted this from 1512–14, with the bulk of the subjects chosen by Julius II. On the main wall (to the right) is the *Expulsion of Heliodorus from the Temple at Jerusalem* which alludes to Julius II's success in freeing the States of the Church from foreign powers. On the left is the *Mass at Bolsena* which portrays a miracle that occurred in northern Lazio in 1263, when a piece of Communion bread purportedly began to bleed. On the long wall is *Leo I Repulsing Attila*, which portrays both Raphael and Julius II, and was partly executed by Raphael's assistants. Attila, mounted on a white horse, the Huns behind him, is frozen in fear by a vision of St Peter and St Paul.

On the courtyard wall is the *Liberation of St Peter*, alluding to the capture of Leo X after the battle of Ravenna, in which the French fought the Spanish and papal armies for control of northern Italy.

Vatican Museums
Lower Floor

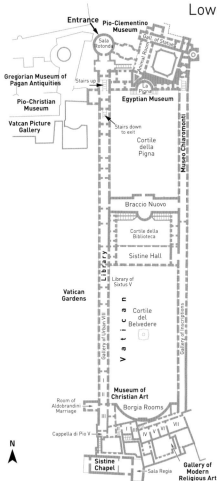

Entrance

Pio-Clementino Museum

Sala Rotonda

Gall. of Statues

Animal Room

Gregorian Museum of Pagan Antiquities

Stairs up

La Pigna

Egyptian Museum

Pio-Christian Museum

Vatcan Picture Gallery

Stairs down to exit

Cortile della Pigna

Museo Chiaromonti

Braccio Nuovo

Cortile della Biblioteca

Sistine Hall

Library

Library of Sixtus V

Vatican Gardens

Gallery of Urban VIII

Vatican

Cortile del Belvedere

Gallery of Inscriptions

Museum of Christian Art

Room of Aldobrandini Marriage

Borgia Rooms

Cappella di Pio V

Sistine Chapel

Sala Regia

Gallery of Modern Religious Art

N

Vatican Museums
Upper Floor

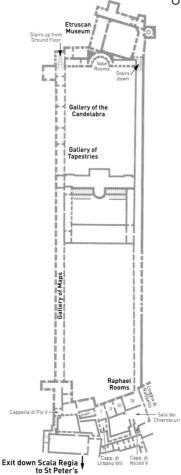

Etruscan Museum

Stairs up from Ground Floor

Vase Rooms

Stairs down

Gallery of the Candelabra

Gallery of Tapestries

Gallery of Maps

Raphael Rooms

Loggia di Raffaello

Cappella di Pio V

I   II   III   IV

Sala dei Chiaroscuri

Capp. di Urbano VIII

Capp. di Nicolò V

Exit down Scala Regia to St Peter's

N

Room II (Stanza della Segnatura): This is where the pope signed papal documents, and has the most beautiful and harmonious frescoes in the series, painted entirely by Raphael from 1508-11. On the long wall opposite the entrance is the famous *Disputation on the Holy Sacrament*. Raphael divides the difficult composition into two parts, making the space appear far larger than it is. Christ appears in the heavenly area between the Virgin and St John the Baptist; above is God the Father surrounded by angels; beneath, the Holy Dove between four angels holding the book of the Gospels. On the far left is Fra' Angelico, in a black Dominican habit, with Bramante in the foreground.

On the wall nearest the Courtyard of the Belvedere is the famous *Parnassus* scene. Apollo is playing the violin in the shade of laurels, surrounded by the nine Muses and the great poets. In the group of poets on the left is the figure of the blind Homer, between Dante and Virgil.

The legendary *School of Athens* symbolises the accomplishments of Philosophy. The setting is a portico, representing the Palace of Science, a magnificent example of Renaissance architecture inspired by Bramante's project for the rebuilding of St Peter's. Here, the greatest philosophers and scholars of all time gather around the two masters: Plato, probably based on Leonardo da Vinci, points towards heaven, symbolising his speculative philosophical system; and Aristotle towards earth, denoting his scientific approach. Raphael stares straight out of the fresco on the lower right. The figure leaning on the block at the front is thought to be Michelangelo as Heraclitus, the first Western philosopher to establish a concrete system of thought, perhaps demonstrating Raphael's deep respect for another of the great Renaissance geniuses, who was working on the Sistine chapel at the time.

Room I (Stanza dell'Incendio): On the ceiling is the *Glorification of the Holy Trinity* by Perugino, Raphael's master, the only work not destroyed when Raphael took over the decoration of these rooms. Facing the window is the Incendio di Borgo, depicting the fire that raged through Rome in 847, and was miraculously put out when the pope made the sign of the Cross at the flames.

BORGIA ROOMS

The Borgia apartment is decorated with important frescoes by Pinturicchio and his studio (1492–94), which celebrate the purportedly divine origins of the Borgia. The Spanish family was notorious in Rome, and rumours abounded of all kinds of infamy, including incest and murder. The rooms were abandoned after 1503 until 1889, when Pope Leo XIII had them restored and opened to the public.

THE SISTINE CHAPEL

The building takes its name from Pope Sixtus IV, who commissioned the construction of the chapel in 1475 to provide a new and grander location for papal ceremony and for the assembly of the conclave that elected a new pope. The relative proportions of its design (40.5m by 13.2m by 20.7m high) are those given for Solomon's temple in *I Kings 6*, v. 2. Its appearance and dimensions also recall the ancient Curia in the Roman Forum (*see p. 32*).

The 15th-century paintings (1481–83)

Sixtus commissioned Perugino, one of the finest masters of painting technique then alive, to supervise work on the Chapel, carried out by, among others, Botticelli and Pinturicchio. The most beautiful fresco (fifth from the altar on the left-hand wall) is *Christ Giving the Keys to St Peter*, painted by Perugino. The painting cycle was deliberately conceived to legitimise papal authority, with Moses and Christ entrusting St Peter with the keys to the Kingdom of Heaven and thus, ancestrally, to the pope. The Classical, circular building in the background can be seen as a forerunner of the new ideals which the Renaissance would bring to architecture, while the Arch of Constantine is another depiction of papal authority, this time granted by the Imperial state.

The ceiling (1508–12)

The decoration of the Sistine Chapel is rightly held as one of mankind's greatest individual artistic achievements. It represents a new beginning for Western art, after which the heights of antiquity could be matched, or even bettered. Michelangelo was 33 when he received the commission from Pope Julius II to paint the chapel's

a/s/e Rome

ceiling. The original commission was to paint the 12 apostles as well as ornamental motifs, but when Michelangelo complained that this was an uninspiring topic, the pontiff handed over full control of the project to the artist.

The ceiling covers an area of some 500m square, and to carry out this mammoth task Michelangelo devised a scaffolding structure which supported him close to the ceiling surface while he worked in bands from side to side. He began at the eastern end—where his figures are smaller—towards the altar end, where he appears to have gained confidence and mastered the issue of scale. Today we can see the paintings in their original glory, as Michelangelo and his contemporaries would have seen them, after the extensive cleaning programme of 1981–94.

Nine episodes were chosen to illustrate early chapters from Genesis along the centre of the ceiling, within a powerful trompe l'oeil architectural framework, and nude figures at their sides. Below these sit enthroned prophets and sibyls, seemingly operating in a different realm of time and space. Episodes in the history of the salvation of the people of Israel are portrayed in the corners.

Key to the ceiling frescoes

[1] David and Goliath
[2] Zechariah
[3] Judith and Holofernes
[4] Joel
[5] Drunkenness of Noah
[6] Delphic Sibyl
[7] Zerubbabel
[8] The Flood
[9] Josiah
[10] Eritrean Sibyl
[11] The Sacrifice of Noah
[12] Isaiah
[13] Uzziah
[14] Expulsion from Paradise
[15] Hezekiah
[16] Ezekiel
[17] Creation of Eve

[18] Cumaean Sibyl
[19] Rehoboam
[20] Creation of Adam
[21] Asa
[22] Persian Sibyl
[23] Separation of Land from Water
[24] Daniel
[25] Salmon
[26] Creation of Sun, Moon and Stars
[27] Jesse
[28] Jeremiah
[29] Separation of Light from Darkness
[30] Libyan Sibyl

[1]	[2]	[3]
[4]	[5]	[6]
[7]	[8]	[9]
[10]	[11]	[12]
[13]	[14]	[15]
[16]	[17]	[18]
[19]	[20]	[21]
[22]	[23]	[24]
[25]	[26]	[27]
[28]	[29]	[30]

The *Last Judgement* (1535–41)

On the wall above the altar, this fresco, the largest of the Renaissance era, was painted in gloomier times than the rest of the ceiling, unveiled 29 years earlier: after the tribulations of the Reformation as well as the devastating Sack of Rome in 1527. The powerful figure of Christ, looking more like a Greek god than a Jewish prophet, is the hub of the whole circular composition: He compels the dead on His right to rise, and damns those to His left. The saints swarming in the rich blue background around him seem to demand justice for the sinners at the bottom of the picture. The fresco ushers in the new era of Mannerism, an artistic style that moved away from the Classicism typified by the chapel's ceiling and Raphael's *School of Athens* nearby. The *Last Judgement* was intended as the culmination of the Sistine Chapel's attempt to tell the Christian history of the world. A controversial work, it was equally condemned for its nudity (the draperies were a later addition) as it was praised for its artistry.

You can leave the tour of the Museums here by descending Bernini's Scala Regia to St Peter's (except Wed), or you can continue to the Museum of Christian Art and the Vatican Library by leaving via a small door in the north wall of the nave.

CHIARAMONTI MUSEUM & NEW WING

This magnificent ancient sculpture collection is displayed in Bramante's east corridor and was arranged by Antonio Canova. Highlights include a first century sepulchral monument of Nonnius Zethus and his family at Section X, a square marble block with eight cavities for the remains of his family members. In Section XVI the *Head of Athena* is a copy of a 5th-century original. The whites of the eyes were probably made of ivory, the pupils of semi-precious stones, and the eyelashes of bronze.

Continuing to the right is the New Wing (*Braccio Nuovo*), which holds some of the most valuable ancient sculptures in the Vatican. The *Augustus of Prima Porta* (*see right*) is the quintessential portrait of the Emperor, in which he is portrayed as a young man, as was customary. It was found in his wife's villa at Prima Porta, 12km north of Rome, in 1863. The statue originally held a bronze sceptre or lance in his left hand, while his raised right hand shows him about to address his troops. When it was discovered it still bore traces of colour which showed that his cloak was once painted deep purple, while the reliefs on his breastplate were light blue and purple. In fact, most Greek and Roman statues were multi-coloured in order to increase their impact and legibility from a distance. Just before the recess there is a statue of the respected Emperor Titus, who ruled from 79–81. A bust of Julius Caesar dates from the time of Augustus, and another from the late Republican era, is thought to be a portrait of Mark Antony. Other highlights are the *Wounded Amazon*, a sculpture of the Nile and the *Resting Satyr*.

The *Augustus of Prima Porta* in the Chiaramonti Museum

PIO-CLEMENTINO MUSEUM

This museum, with its wonderful collection of Greek and Roman sculptures was founded by Pius VI in the 18th century and is named after him and his predecessor, Clement XIV. The contents of the sculpture galleries are mainly Greek and Roman originals, or Roman copies of Greek originals executed in the 1st and 2nd centuries. In the 16th century Pope Paul IV decided that the male sculptures should be covered with a fig leaf.

Gabinetto dell'Apoxyomenos: This room is named after the statue of a finely honed athlete using a strigil to scrape oil from his body. It is a copy of a Greek bronze original which was the masterpiece of Lysippus (c. 330 BC) and illustrates the increase in realism in Greek art of this era.

Octagonal courtyard of the Belvedere: Here, there are four corner recesses, each of which contains a masterpiece from antiquity. Moving clockwise from the entrance they are as follows:

(1) Gabinetto dell'Apollo: This recess holds the *Apollo Belvedere*, a second-century Roman copy of a bronze original (4th century BC). It was found in the 15th century and has epitomised Western aesthetic ideals ever since, and was considered a key sight on the Roman leg of any Grand Tour. Bernini was inspired by this ancient work when he sculpted his *Apollo and Daphne,* which is exhibited at the Galleria and Museo Borghese (*see p. 84*).

(2) Gabinetto del Laocoönte: This recess contains the famous group of *Laocoön* and his two sons in the coils of the serpents, (*see right*) a striking illustration of the story told by Virgil in the *Aeneid.* Laocoön, priest of Apollo, famously said, '*Do not trust the Horse, Trojans. Whatever it is, I fear the Greeks even bearing gifts.*' He was right, as either Apollo or Athene sent serpents to kill Laocoön and his young sons. The violent realism, skill and detail all typify late-Hellenistic sculpture.

(3) Gabinetto dell' Hermes: The work here is a copy of an original by Praxiteles and shows Hermes, the bringer of souls to the Underworld. It has stood in this spot since the collection began.

(4) Gabinetto del Canova: Here are three Neoclassical statues: *Perseus* (inspired by the *Apollo Belvedere*) and *Creugas* and *Damoxenes* by Canova, placed here when Napoleon looted the bulk of the Classical masterpieces in 1800.

VATICAN PICTURE GALLERY

The Vatican Picture Gallery (*Pinacoteca Vaticana*) lies in the opposite direction to the beginning of the 'Sistine Route' and is therefore happily devoid of crowds. The gallery is devoted mostly to Italian painters, and outstanding amongst the collection are:

Laocoön and his sons writhing against serpents in the Pio-Clementino Museum

Room III: The two beautiful panels by Fra' Angelico depict scenes from the life of St Nicholas of Bari, and formed part of a polyptych painted for a Dominican church in Perugia c. 1437. A Dominican friar, the artist received his name—*angelic brother*—due to his saintly painting skills. The *Virgin with Child* is also by him.

Room VIII: This room contains three of Raphael's most famous paintings. The *Coronation of the*

Virgin was his first large composition, painted at just 20 years old in Perugia, in 1503. The *Madonna of Foligno* is from c. 1511. The *Transfiguration* is Raphael's last work: the scene depicts the dramatic episode of the curing of a young man possessed of a devil and was commissioned for Narbonne Cathedral in 1517.

Room IX: *St Jerome* (c. 1480), one of the least known but most haunting works by Leonardo da Vinci, is hung here. It is an early work which was left unfinished: the lion in the foreground is only lightly sketched. Leonardo's method was to leave the foreground till last. The head and torso are testament to the artist's deep knowledge of anatomy and show just a thin layer of skin covering the saint's muscles and bones. At some point the painting was sawn in two and was not restored until the 19th century.

Room XII: The powerful *Descent from the Cross* (1602) by Caravaggio (copied by Rubens) is displayed here. The *Crucifixion of St Peter* was painted by Guido Reni in 1604-05, and shows the influence of Caravaggio's painting in the church of Santa Maria del Popolo.

Castel Sant'Angelo *(open 9–7, closed Mon, entry fee, Tel: 06 681 9111, guided tours of parts of the castle normally closed to the public are available often on Sat and Sun, booking necessary).* Castel Sant'Angelo is the imposing circular structure that faces the Tiber and is visible from much of the city. It was begun by Hadrian in 134, as a mausoleum for himself and his family. It was later secured by defensive walls and became Rome's citadel in the Middle Ages. It has also been used as a prison, and the philosopher Giordano Bruno was held here for six years, accused of heresy. Today, it houses a museum containing 16th-century stuccoes and frescoes and a collection of paintings and tapestries. Highlights are the Mausoleum of Hadrian itself, approached by a ramp which survives from ancient times, and the Courtyard of the Angel on the second floor where

The Bernini-designed bridge crosses the Tiber to Castel Sant'Angelo

you can see Michelangelo's façade of the Medici chapel (c. 1514), built for Leo X. From the ramparts there are wonderful views of Rome and the Tiber. **Map p. 120, B4**

Ponte Sant'Angelo. The pedestrian bridge leading across the Tiber to the entrance of Castel Sant'Angelo is a fitting approach to the castle. The ten magnificent statues of angels were designed by Bernini and executed in 1688 by his pupils, including Ercole Ferrata. Each of the angels holds an instrument of the Passion of Christ: the Column against which Christ was whipped, and the Whip used prior to His crucifixion; the Crown of Thorns placed on Christ's head; the Cross on which He was crucified; the inscription I.N.R.I placed on the Cross declaring Christ the 'King of the Jews'; the Nails used for the crucifixion; a piece of cloth Christ wore when He was crucified; the Spear used to pierce Christ's side to prove He was dead; the vinegar soaked Sponge used to stanch Christ's wounds; and the Dice thrown by the soldiers to bid for Christ's clothing. Today, the bridge is crowded with groups of vendors selling cheap handbags and crafts. **Map p. 120, C4**

The Vatican City and Gardens (*open for guided tours only: 10am Tues, Thurs, Sat; entry fee, Tel: 06 6988 4676, booking essential one day in advance from the Vatican museum entrance*). The walled Città del Vaticano spans 44 hectares (less than half a square kilometre), holds a population of around 550 and, in terms of size, is the world's smallest independent state. As such, it has its own postal service, currency and radio station. The Swiss Guard have policed the Vatican City since 1506, and retain the unusual uniform said to have been designed by Michelangelo.

The Vatican Gardens were laid out in the 16th century on the site of the martyrdom of early Christians. Opposite the west end of St Peter's is the compact Santo Stefano degli Abissini, built by Leo III (795–816) and given to Coptic monks in 1479. To the south is the Vatican's railway station, sadly seldom used. At the west of the city is a reproduction of the Grotto of Lourdes, presented to Leo XIII by French Catholics. Near here is the old Vatican radio station (no longer broadcasting), designed by Guglielmo Marconi. **Map p. 120, B2–C2**

eat

The Vatican City is the most visited district of Rome but the best food on offer seems to be spiritual rather than gastronomic. However, there are some restaurants to be found in the business district, particularly along the streets leading off Via Ottaviano, where you will be rewarded with pleasant service and a delicious meal. Borgo Pio, close to St Peter's Square, is an atmospheric street lined with restaurants catering to visitors from every part of the world. For price categories, see p. 9.

RESTAURANTS

1 €€€ Il Simposio, *Piazza Cavour 16, Tel: 06 321 1502*. You are guaranteed a good selection of wine at this restaurant attached to the city's largest wine shop (Il Constantino) and at the back of a popular *enoteca* (wine bar): the restaurant carries a list of 20 wines by the glass and over 500 by the bottle. Fortunately, the food at Il Simposio is just as sophisticated and the owners have expanded widely on the simple snacks usually served as an accompaniment to the wine in a typical *enoteca*, to offer modern interpretations of classic Roman dishes. The helpful staff will recommend a wine to compliment any dish, even the 'chocolate oblivion' pudding. **Map p. 120, B4**

2 €€€ La Veranda dell'Hotel Columbus, *Borgo Santo Spirito 73, Tel: 06 687 2973*. You will dine in splendour at La Veranda, housed in the historical Palazzo della Rovere,

frescoed by Pinturrichio. The palazzo was built in 1480 for Pope Sixtus IV's (the founder of the Sistine Chapel) nephew in an area of the city which was being radically modernised to accommodate the swelling number of pilgrims to St Peter's. Today, the restaurant is part of the elegant Hotel Columbus and has a dining room in the beautifully decorated former refectory, or, in the warmer months, out in the private courtyard garden. Some highlights on the menu include *fiori di zucca in tempura farciti di mazzancolle* (zucchini flowers stuffed with prawns) and the *spigola con mozzarella di bufala, radicchio trevigiano e pepe verde* (sea bass, buffalo's mozzarella, red chicory and green pepper). It is advisable to book in advance. **Map p. 120, C3**

3 €€ L'Arcangelo, *Via Giuseppe Gioacchino Belli 59/61, Tel: 06 321 0992*. A very pleasant restaurant decorated in the style of a 50s tavern with simple dark wood panelling, tiled floor and crisp white tablecloths. L'Arcangelo is close to the Castel Sant'Angelo and a ten-minute walk from St Peter's making it easy to visit as a lunch destination between the two sights, or an alternative to the evening dining scene of the Navona district, just across Ponte Umberto. **Map p. 120, B4**

④ € Il Matriciano, *Via dei Gracchi 55, T: 06 321 3040.* A spacious, light restaurant close to the Vatican museums. In a district populated more by businessmen and women than visitors, the restaurant is a haven of quiet and calm after the queues and crowds around the Vatican. The service is courteous and friendly and food is served

quickly. Excellent antipasti include *prosciutto di Parma*, which is freshly carved by the waiter, and *carciofo alla Romana* (artichoke stuffed with mint and garlic), while the *bucatini alla Matriciana* (hollow spaghetti in a tomato, bacon and hot pepper sauce) is typically Roman, and makes for a delicious light lunch. **Map p. 120, A3**

⑤ € Osteria dell'Angelo, *Via G. Bettolo 24, Tel: 06 372 9470.* An excellent osteria which has been offering strictly Roman-only dishes for many years and established a league of loyal diners. Local classics such as *tonnerelli cacio e pepe* (pasta with cheese and pepper) and *penne alla pajata* (pasta with intestines) are typical of the daily specials. **Map p. 120, A2**

CAFÉS & ICE CREAM

⑥ Gelateria Pellachia, *Via Cola di Rienzo 103.* Not only is this the best *gelateria* in the area, it also has an enduring history. During the early 1900s the owner, Giovanni Pellachia, kept his own cow at the shop in order to provide fresh milk for his ice cream. The quality of the ice-cream gained such a reputation that the *gelateria* was even kept running during World War II when rationing was notorious for the demise of many eating establishments. The cow may now be gone but the ingredients are still fresh and Giovanni's grandson, who has taken over, keeps their products as

simple and natural as in his grandfather's day. **Map p. 120, A4**

⑦ Sciascia dal 1922, *Via Fabbio Massimo 80.* An excellent coffee bar which roasts its own coffee as well as importing beans from all over the world. The staff are particularly friendly and will be happy to help you choose from the wide range of roasts to make up your cappuccino or *caffè ristretto*. There are also delicious pastries to accompany the coffee, particularly good are the *cornetti*, a traditional breakfast pastry, but good as a snack at any time of day. **Map p. 120, A4**

Coffee in Rome

Coffee is an essential part of the daily Roman routine, fuelling a frantic city that would surely grind to a halt in its absence. Romans are genuine coffee aficionados, and there are hundreds of small, independent establishments which serve exquisite stuff, mainly made from the full flavoured, low-caffeine, Arabica bean variety. However, the range of coffee drinks available is vast and which to ask for and how is a delicate art.

The basic coffee is *un caffè*, (espresso), which is a richly-flavoured and intense caffeine hit, and serves as the basis for numerous other permutations. Espresso is served in a small cup or *al ventro* (in a glass) and drunk in two or three sips at most, particularly after dinner. Variations include *caffè ristretto* (extra strong) and *caffè corretto* (a coffee 'corrected' with a shot of whisky, brandy or grappa). *Lungo* (long) and *americano* are weaker variants with hot water, while an *espresso doppio* is a double. A *caffè macchiato* ('stained coffee') is an espresso with a small amount of frothy milk, and is not to be confused with a *latte macchiato*, which is hot milk with a dash of espresso.

Cappuccino (literally meaning 'little hat', from its covering of thick, frothy milk) is probably the best-travelled coffee in the world. In Italy it is almost considered a meal in itself, so locals tend not to order one after 11am. A Roman cappuccino is served lukewarm, so that it can be consumed quickly whilst standing at the bar. One good reason to follow suit is that your coffee will cost significantly more if you are seated, especially in more touristy locales. Variations include *cappuccino senza schiuma,* which is without foam and also known as *caffè latte.*

A refreshing Roman summertime speciality is the *caffè latte freddo,* which is a cold espresso with cold milk, and usually has a sweet and intense flavour—ask for it *senza zucchero* if you don't require sugar. One notable peculiarity is the *caffè d'orzo,* which is a caffeine-free coffee substitute made from barley, and if it's getting late and you have a busy day of sightseeing in the morning, maybe one of these, or a *caffè decaffeinato,* is your best option.

shop

The Vatican City is not known for its shopping opportunities but unsurprisingly it has the biggest supply of religious souvenirs in the city, and the streets surrounding St Peter's are a perfect place to escape the queues and do some souvenir hunting. There are also some good markets to pick up fresh food for picnics as well as some excellent grocery shops selling Italian and international delicacies. Before Cardinal Ratzinger became Pope Benedict XVI, these were his local neighbourhood shops for 25 years.

Via Cola di Rienzo (**map p. 120, A3–A4**), with its wide pavements, is a popular shopping destination for locals and families to promenade at the weekend. It can easily be reached from Piazza del Popolo by crossing the Tiber, and there are many fashion stores here, which sell shoes, bags and other accessories.

Rome's largest **Castroni** store is situated at no. 196. It is a haven for Italian specialities such as *peperoncino* (chilli chocolate), black seppia pasta, and international foodstuffs: English jams and marmalades sit alongside sections of Oriental, Arab, Middle Eastern, Jewish and Mexican cuisines. Homesick Americans will be happy to find pancakes, chocolate pies and various coffees here. Best of all though is the bar, serving Italian cakes and various freshly ground coffees, some of which are house-produced, and can be taken home. Next door,

at no. 200, is the gourmet grocery **Franchi**, which shouldn't be missed if you intend to bring home some porcini mushrooms, Parma ham or other specialities, which they will vacuum pack for you. Franchi is a feast for the eyes and the palate, and you can also stop here for a three-course standing lunch.

The department store **Coin**, at no. 200/204, has a large supermarket in the basement, handy for picnics.

A large, picturesque **covered market** stands on the same street, spanning the block from Via Fabio Massimo to Piazza de Unita (**map p. 120, A4–A3**). Inside, you will find a good variety of fresh produce. The building was constructed in 1928 and the main facade has an impressive arched entrance while two fountains decorate the sides. Also popular is the **Trionfale market**, near the Vatican Museum on Via Andrea Doria (**map p. 120, A2**), with a superb variety of grocery

Holy souvenirs in the Vatican shopping district of Borgo Pio

stores for Romans and visitors. The prices are reasonable here, compared to other stores in the area. **Borgo Pio** (map p. 120, B3) is the most picturesque street in the Borgo area and is *the* place to buy rosary beads, miniature statues and postcards. The current pope, Benedict XVI, lived in this area when he first came to Rome in 1981 to take the role of prefect of the congregation, and chose to stay in this area rather than the apartment traditionally offered to holders of the post. In the afternoons the then Cardinal Ratzinger would often go out for a walk along the streets near his apartment and would stop to speak with the shop-keepers along the Borgo Pio. One fruit-seller recalls how once the homesick cardinal asked him which apples were best for a strudel, while an electrician speaks of the time that they spoke 'just as if we were old friends' after he went to the cardinal's flat to fix a problem. Cardinal Ratzinger remained living in this district until he became pope in 2005.

art glossary

Algardi, Alessandro (1598–1654) Italian sculptor, architect and draughts-man who was considered to be, with Gian Lorenzo Bernini, one of Rome's key sculptors in the mid-17th century, representing a Classical alternative to Bernini's Baroque works.

Baroque Style of art that dominated the 17th century, and closely associated with the Counter-Reformation (see below). The ethos of the Baroque is sensual, theatrical and dramatic, seeking to create an emotional rather than intellectual response in the viewer. In Rome, Guido Reni's works represent early Baroque painting. In architecture, Pietro da Cortona, Bernini and Borromini excelled.

Bernini, Gian Lorenzo (1598–1680) Sculptor, architect and painter of the 17th century and a vital influence on the development of the Italian Baroque style (see box on p. 83).

Borromini, Francesco (1599–1667) Architect who spent his working life in Rome, and became a great rival to Bernini. His standing as one of the great architects of the Baroque era, with an innovative and intricate geometrical style, came only after his suicide. Notable Borromini works in Rome include Sant'Agnese in Agone (see p. 101) and Palazzo Barberini (see p. 60).

Bramante, Donato (1444–1514) Architect and painter who studied painting from an early age. When he moved to Rome in 1499, Bramante caught the attention of the future Pope Julius II, who engaged him in the renewal of the Vatican complex four years later. Bramante worked on St Peter's (see p.122) for the majority of his time in Rome.

Canova, Antonio (1757–1822) Rome's most inventive and celebrated neo-Classicist sculptor. Also a painter and architect. His masterpieces include Pauline Bonaparte as *Venus* in the Galleria Borghese (see p. 82), and *Hercules and Lichas* at the Galleria Nazionale D'Arte Moderna (see p. 88).

Caravaggio (Michelangelo Merisi; 1571–1610) One of Italy's most celebrated artists and the first great figure of the Baroque era. (see box on p. 103).

Carrà, Carlo (1881–1966) Italian painter and one of the prominent members of the Futurist Movement in the early 20th century, before becoming influenced by Giorgio de Chirico and his Metaphysical works, and later the Novecento art movement.

Carracci, Annibale (1560–1609) Considered one of the greatest Italian painters of his era. He was key in the evolution of the 'ideal' classical landscape, and is generally believed to have invented caricature.

Cavallini, Pietro (active 1250–1330) Italian painter and mosaicist who carried out large-scale fresco and mosaic works in many of the city's basilicas and churches. He was fortunate enough to reach artistic maturity just as the Papacy was undertaking large-scale artistic projects. His frescoes can be seen in Santa Maria in Aracoeli (see p. 27).

Chiaroscuro Italian term used to describe bold contrasts between light and shade in art. Leonardo da Vinci was a pioneer of this technique but it is the 17th-century artists with whom the term is most associated, including Caravaggio.

Chirico, Giorgio de (1888–1978) Influential Metaphysical painter whose work inspired the Surrealist Movement of the early 20th century. Born in Greece, he lived and worked throughout Europe before settling in Rome in 1944. Many of his paintings can be seen in his former apartment (see p. 77).

Classical art Art of ancient Greece and Rome. In sculpture and painting, the Classical style sought to attain perfection of realism and form: an 'ideal' human beauty and an 'ideal' nature. In architecture, it regarded mathematics as divine, and attempted to achieve a perfect geometrical harmony within the structure of its buildings. Classicism and the ideas and style of Classical art re-emerged during the Italian Renaissance, and still remain a major influence in European culture.

Correggio (Antonio Allegri; 1489–1534) The foremost painter of the Parma school who prefigured Rococo art by several centuries with his use of dynamic composition and illusionistic perspective. He was enigmatic, both as an artist and a man, and never studied under a master, thus often making it difficult to identify a stylistic link between his works.

Cosmatesque Medieval style of mosaic decoration (see box on p. 28).

Counter-Reformation Response by the Roman Catholic church to the Protestant Reformation, which sought to reform the abuses of Catholicism and challenged its spiritual domination of the Western world. The Mother Church responded with a magnificent display of splendour, wealth and power, an emotional appeal to the senses. The Baroque style of art and architecture was born.

Etruscan An ancient civilization that existed north of Rome from pre-historic times. This polytheistic society had its own language, government, mythology and religion, which was highly influenced by the preceding Greek system of beliefs. Many intriguing artworks survive from this era, most notably the bronze She-wolf of Rome in the Palazzo dei Conservatori on the Capitoline Hill (see p. 23).

Fattori, Giovanni (1825–1908) Italian painter and etcher of landscapes with figures. The group of painters to which Fattori later belonged became known as the Macchiaioli School. A late-bloomer, he produced many outstanding etchings of rural subjects towards the end of his life. Several of his works can be seen at the Galleria Nazionale D'Arte Moderna (see p. 88).

Ferrata, Ercole (1610–86) Sculptor at an early age, and whose early works were heavily influenced by his classmate Alessandro Algardi. Ferrata also sculpted, under Bernini's guidance, the *Angel with a Cross* for the Ponte Sant'Angelo (see p. 140).

Fontana, Domenico (1543–1607) Architect and engineer who settled in Rome and worked for the future Pope Sixtus V. He made his name towards the end of the 16th century by re-erecting Egyptian obelisks in front of St Peter's Basilica (see p. 121), and St John Lateran (see p. 43). He also built the Vatican Library and supervised the erection of the dome of St Peter's.

Fra' Angelico (c. 1395–1455) Painter, illuminator and Dominican friar. He emerged from humble beginnings and was highly innovative in his fresco projects for the Vatican (see p. 106), softening the Tuscan style of mural painting with his own colourful and luminescent touches. He is buried at Santa Maria sopra Minerva (see p. 106).

Fresco From the Italian word meaning 'fresh', a technique of painting directly onto wet plaster on a wall; the technique is extremely durable in dry climates. The ceiling of the Sistine Chapel (see p. 131) is one of the most famous frescoes in Rome.

Fuga, Ferdinando (1699–1781) Florentine architect who spent much of his time working in Rome. His masterwork is the Neoclassical façade of Santa Maria Maggiore (see p. 52).

Futurism Early 20th-century modern art movement that arose out of Italy, whose art expressed a love of movement, machines and the modern world. Carlo Carrà was one of its leading figures.

Giacomo della Porta (1539–1602) Chief Roman architect during the late 16th century who worked on many important buildings in Rome, including St. Peter's Basilica and the Sforza Chapel in Santa Maria Maggiore (see p. 55).

Leonardo da Vinci (1452–1519) The prototypical Renaissance man who had a colossal effect on art, and was a diversely talented artist. His theories were the touchstone for artistic representation and expression across Europe for four centuries, and he established the standards for figure draughtsmanship, handling of light, shade, space and landscapes, as well as character and narrative, and in doing so radically shifted the boundaries of art.

Lippi, Filippino (1457–1504) Florentine son of a nun and a Carmelite monk and painter, Filippino became one of the leading artists of the late 15th century. He moved to Rome in 1488, where he was entrusted with the decoration of the Carafa Chapel in Santa Maria sopra Minerva (see p. 106).

Macchiaioli School Group of Tuscan painters who were active in the mid-19th century, who believed in painting outdoors to capture natural light and colours, and whose paintings were characterised by spots of colour (macchie). Because of this they are often called the Tuscan Impressionists. Telemaco Signorini and Giovanni Fattori were leading artists of this School.

Maderno, Carlo (1556–1629) Maderno is remembered as one of the fathers of Baroque architecture. His façades of St. Peter's Basilica and other Roman churches were of key importance in the development of the Italian Baroque style. Pope Paul V appointed him chief architect of St. Peter's in 1603.

Mannerism Period in art history that followed the High Renaissance, and dominated most of the 1500s. The term relates to the 'manner' or individual style of the artists of this period, as their art became more experimental.

Many artists believed that the perfection that Classicism had striven for could not be developed further after Raphael and Leonardo, so artists began to play with the rules of Classicism. Idealised human forms and poses became exaggerated, colours became more unusual, highly ordered compositions gave way to irrational space and unnatural lighting.

Michelangelo Buonarroti (1475–1564) Sculptor, painter, architect, poet and engineer, whose huge contribution to the Renaissance was only rivalled by Leonardo da Vinci. One of Michelangelo's best-known sculptures, the *Pietà* (see p. 124) was sculpted before he was 30. Despite his low opinion of painting, Michelangelo also created two of the most influential fresco paintings in the history of Western art, namely the *Last Judgement* and the ceiling of the Sistine Chapel in the Vatican (see p. 131–133). Later in his life he designed the dome of St Peter's. Other fine examples of his work are the statue of *Moses* in San Pietro in Vincoli (see p. 38) and *The Risen Christ* in Santa Maria sopra Minerva (see p. 106).

Neoclassicism Style of art and architecture that arose in response to increased travel by northern Europeans to see the antiquities of Greece and Rome, and also as a rejection of the stagey excess of the Baroque and the flouncy frivolity of its successor, Rococo. Neoclassicism aspired to a serene purity of form and line, and a rational rather than emotional approach to subject matter. Antonio Canova is Italy's finest Neoclassical artist.

Novecento art Art of the 'nine hundreds' i.e. the 20th century. Novecento art was a reaction against European avant-garde movements such as Art Nouveau in favour of a more ordered, rational and Classical style.

Perugino (Pietro Vannucci; 1446–1523) A major contributor to the advancements in painting from the style of the early Renaissance to the High Renaissance. Through his famous pupil Raphael, his trademark Idealized human figures and spatial composition spread throughout Europe.

Pietro da Cortona (Pietro Berrettini; 1596–1669) Prolific artist and architect of the High Baroque, best known for painting ceiling frescoes, particularly his masterpiece, an allegory of Divine Providence at the Palazzo Barberini (see p. 60). He was also a skilled architect, but suffered somewhat from living in the shade cast by Bernini and Borromini.

Pinturicchio (Bernardino di Betto; 1454–1513) Italian painter who collaborated on the Sistine Chapel with Perugino, quickly establishing his reputation as a painter of idiosyncratic and picturesque decorative cycles. His most important commissions included the decoration of the Borgia Rooms in the Vatican (*see p. 131*).

Polyptych A work of art, usually a panel painting, which is divided into four or more sections, hinged together, each usually dipicting a different scene. In such works the whole is intended to be greater than the sum of its parts, as the pictures tell a story, or have a related theme.

Ponzio, Flaminio (1560–1613) Architect during the Mannerist period. After training in Milan, he moved to Rome, where he worked briefly with Domenico Fontana and for Pope Paul V. He designed the Borghese Chapel for the Pope in Santa Maria Maggiore (*see p. 55*).

Rainaldi, Carlo (1611–91) Architect from an artistic family, involved with some of the most impressive architectural projects in Rome in the 17th century, meanwhile developing a highly individual version of the Roman High Baroque style. Construction of Sant'Agnese in Agone (*see p. 101*) started under his planning in 1652.

Raphael (Rafaello Sanzio; 1483–1520) Famous painter of Madonnas and noted for his intricate but flamboyant work in the Vatican (*see p. 126*). Raphael was the youngest of the great trio of Italian High Renaissance artists, the others being Leonardo and Michelangelo. His early death at the age of 37 plunged the art world into deep mourning.

Renaissance (meaning 'rebirth') A period of massive cultural change in Europe that originated in Florence in the late Middle Ages and lasted until the 16th century. Ancient Greek and Roman texts which had been lost in the West but survived in Byzantium and in Arabic translations, were 'rediscovered', which sparked a great thirst for Classical learning. Renaissance artists strove for an increased realism in sculpture and painting (particularly the depiction of space and perspective), and were patronised by wealthy ruling families and the Church.

Reni, Guido (1575–1642) Celebrated and influential 17th-century Italian painter, whose sophistication dominated the Bolognese school. Influenced by Raphael and Greco-Roman art, he captured Idealized beauty with compositional and figural poise. His religious art was concerned with the expression of extreme emotion and pathos. An excellent example in Rome is his *St Sebastian* in the Pinacoteca Capitolina (*see p. 24*).

Rococo Art form which emerged from early 18th-century France as a progression from Baroque. It was characterised by sumptuousness, light-heartedness and elegance, in contrast to Baroque's darker colours and more weighty themes. Rococo paintings often depict natural settings and centre on the upper-class life and light-hearted romance, rather than religious or heroic topics. The style was superseded by Neoclassicism in the latter half of the 18th century.

Rubens, Sir Peter Paul (1577–1640) Flemish artist of the highest order, accredited with moving European art forward with his merging of the elaborate creativity of the Italian Renaissance with the Flemish Realism he grew up with. Rubens spent eight years in Rome and during his stay was significantly influenced by both Caravaggio and Carracci.

Signorini, Telemaco (1835–1901) Painter, critic and member of the Macchiaioli group (*see above*), producing landscapes, seascapes and Tuscan street scenes. As a critic he was the most passionate spokesman for the Macchiaioli, and wrote humorously on the art world of the latter half of the 19th century.

Titian (Tiziano Vecellio; c. 1485–1576) The greatest artist of the Venetian School, and a towering figure of the Renaissance, known for his use of colour, which is sumptuous and thoughtful by turns. He worked for many illustrious figures including Emperor Charles V and his son Philip II of Spain. His early style is represented in his masterpiece *Sacred and Profane Love* in the Borghese Gallery (*see p. 86*)

Trompe l'oeil (meaning 'trick of the eye' in French) Artistic effect where a flat image is painted to give the illusion of being three dimensional. It is popularly used on ceilings where the images appear to reach up into a concave vaulted space.

Velázquez, Diego (1599–1660) The finest painter of the Spanish School and one of the greatest portraitists in the world. A friend of Rubens, he was encouraged to travel to Italy, which he did twice, spending most of his time in Rome. On his second visit in 1648–51 he painted his unsurpassed portrait of Pope Innocent X in the Galleria Doria Pamphilj (*see p. 56 & 58*).

index

Numbers in italics are picture references. Numbers in bold denote major references.

Cover photo by Rianne van Mourik

Photographs by Róbert Szabó Benke (pp. 2, 9, 39, 47, 65, 76, 77, 91, 93, 96, 112, 115, 117, 124, 145); Daniel Nolan (pp. 3, 33, 45, 87, 111); Phil Robinson (pp. 48, 73, 100); Annabel Barber (pp. 19, 25, 63); Robert Aichinger (p. 107); Arion (p. 135); Mario Bélanger (p. 105); Julio Cid González (p. 137); Tom Howells (p. 29); Maria Kaloudi (p. 118); Kursad Keteci (p. 121); Helen McGrath (p. 37); Frank O'Connor (p. 108); Jon Smith (p. 139)

Other images courtesy of Arti Doria Pamphilj (pp. 56, 58); Alinari Archives, Florence (pp. 78, 82); Bridgeman/Alinari Archives (pp. 61, 133); Bridgeman Art Library (p. 23); the Irish Dominican Fathers, San Clemente (p. 42); Hassler Roma (p. 11); Royal Demeure Hotel Group (p. 12)

art/shop/eat Rome
Fully rewritten second edition 2008

Published by Blue Guides Limited, a Somerset Books Company
49–51 Causton St, London SW1P 4AT
www.artshopeat.com
www.blueguides.com
© Blue Guides Limited
Blue Guides is a registered trademark

ISBN 978-1-905131-20-4

Editor: Sophie Livall
Consulting editor: Annabel Barber

Photo editor: Róbert Szabó Benke
Layout and design: Anikó Kuzmich, Regina Rácz
Maps: Dimap Bt
Floor plans: Imre Bába
Printed in Singapore by Tien Wah Press Pte

Photo credits: p. 159, which forms part of this copyright page

We welcome all comments, corrections and views. We want to hear all
feedback, and as a mark of gratitude we will be happy to send a free copy of
one of our books to anyone providing useable corrections, constructive
criticism, or gross flattery. Please contact us via the website,
www.artshopeat.com.

SOMERSET BOOKS